Short-Term Psychodynamic Therapy with Children in Crisis

In *Short-Term Psychodynamic Therapy with Children in Crisis,* Elisabeth Cleve presents the therapeutic stories of four children who have experienced trauma or are displaying dramatic clinical symptoms such as low self-esteem and anxiety. Exploring the situation between the individual child and the therapist, the therapeutic space and their experiences, each chapter follows the sessions and the progress made, concluding with a follow-up after the end of therapy.

Cleve explores each case as it progresses, emphasizing the inner strength of the children and including the interactions between the therapist and the children's parents. The focus of the psychotherapeutic encounter is in each case to help the child face the trauma, mourn what had been suffered and then move on in life with renewed strength. The final chapters explore the ethics of sharing case material and present Cleve's reflections on working with traumatized children. The book also includes forewords by Lars H. Gustafsson, paediatrician and associate professor of social medicine, and Björn Salomonsson, child psychoanalyst and researcher at Karolinska Institutet in Sweden.

This warm and readable work will be insightful reading for child psychologists and psychotherapists and other clinicians working with children who have experienced trauma. It will also be of interest to readers wishing to learn more about the processes of psychotherapy with children.

Elisabeth Cleve was a psychologist, child psychotherapist and supervisor who worked at the Erica Foundation in Stockholm, Sweden, from the mid-1970s until her untimely death in 2013. Respected as a clinician and well-known as a supervisor, she also wrote several books about the psychotherapeutic process which were acclaimed for their accessible style. Two of her previous books were also translated into English.

Short-Term Psychodynamic Therapy with Children in Crisis

Elisabeth Cleve

Routledge
Taylor & Francis Group
LONDON AND NEW YORK

First published in English 2016
by Routledge
2 Park Square, Milton Park, Abingdon, Oxon OX14 4RN

and by Routledge
605 Third Avenue, New York, NY 10017

Routledge is an imprint of the Taylor & Francis Group, an informa business

British Library Cataloguing in Publication Data
A catalogue record for this book is available from the British Library

Library of Congress Cataloging-in-Publication Data
Names: Cleve, Elisabeth, 1946– author.
Title: Short-term psychodynamic therapy with children in crisis / Elisabeth Cleve.
Other titles: Hur lèange ska hon vara dèod? English
Description: Milton Park, Abingdon, Oxon ; New York, NY : Routledge, 2016.
Identifiers: LCCN 2015037532 | ISBN 9781138951402 (hbk) | ISBN 9781138951419 (pbk) | ISBN 9781315651743 (ebk)
Subjects: LCSH: Psychodynamic psychotherapy for children. | Brief psychotherapy.
Classification: LCC RJ505.P92 C5413 2015 | DDC 618.92/8914—dc23
LC record available at http://lccn.loc.gov/2015037532

ISBN: 978-1-138-95140-2 (hbk)
ISBN: 978-1-138-95141-9 (pbk)
ISBN: 978-1-315-65174-3 (ebk)

Typeset in Times
by Apex CoVantage, LLC

To Alma, Alfred and Harry and the fourth little one

Contents

Foreword by Lars H. Gustafsson

When we work with children in crisis, we are given entrance into a world that exists right here in our midst and yet is unknown to many. In my own work as a paediatrician, I sometimes come to think about the duty or the obligation to bear witness, as it is usually referred to in psychological contexts. We tend to associate the act of witnessing with World War II survivors but the context is much wider. Taking all my experiences with me to the grave without sharing them with others can be perceived as little short of a crime against humanity. If humanity is to make changes for the better, more people must get a chance to know reality as it really is. We need to face the destructive forces both within us and around us. We also need to know more about the life force for survival that pulsates within most of us, not least in children.

My reflections are subjective. However, there are also several objective reasons for telling about the world that is revealed to us. In an open society such as ours, *transparency* is essential. As soon as we create rooms that are hidden from outside view, myths are created about what is going on in there. Rumours are easily spread and can adversely affect everyone involved, in this case both clients and therapists. Rumours are quick to nourish prejudices.

Transparency is important from a scientific point of view as well. Today there is a great demand to have *evidence* cited, evidence that backs up different treatment methods. If a treatment is to be recommended and subsidized with taxpayers' money, there must be scientific documentation showing that the treatment works. The side effects must be confirmed as not too severe. It is equally important that the treatment does not contain ethically questionable elements. It therefore does not suffice to report the results of the treatment. The steps toward obtaining the results, the treatment process itself, must be open and accessible to oversight as well.

In addition, those who end up in difficulty and seek different sorts of treatment have the right to know in advance what the treatment entails and how it will be conducted. More and more emphasis is being placed on the right of the person seeking help to choose the form of treatment. For such a choice to be meaningful and possible, detailed *information* must be available concerning what the different alternatives entail.

The information that comes to the fore in the treatment room has a *political dimension* as well. People who seek our help for their own or for their children's difficulties are individuals. At the same time, these individuals are part of a system, a social context that can be supportive but that can also contribute substantially to unhappiness and impaired health. There are numerous convincing studies showing that children's health, both mental and physical, is highly dependent on the nature of their life conditions. Poverty, loneliness and refugee status as well as the work situation and the health and substance abuse status of the parents are only a few examples of factors that play a role. All of us who meet troubled children inevitably learn a great deal about how society functions for the most vulnerable of these, our fellow human beings. We are thus *obliged* to let others know what we know. Otherwise, how can our knowledge lead to the necessary changes in society?

However, when we decide to share our experiences, we immediately come up against a number of ethical dilemmas. Circumstances that are revealed in the therapy room are seldom spoken about otherwise. Needless to say, this is precisely the point. By shining a light on the darkest corners of the soul, and on what is hidden there, it is possible to disarm destructive forces and to liberate healing processes. The high wall of confidentiality that surrounds therapy is a prerequisite if this sequence of events is going to function. Few children, and likewise few adults, would dare to open themselves to their therapists if they could not trust them beyond any doubt. A patient must be able to trust the therapist to let things presented in the therapy room stay within its confines. Thus we have legislation in support of confidentiality. This is as it should be.

If confidentiality is to be broken, the first and foremost requirement is the patient's informed consent. This means that he or she agrees to let what has been said in therapy be made known to others. However, the patient in such cases must have had a chance to think carefully through the consequences of such a release, both in the short and in the longer term. The therapist has a great responsibility here. It can be difficult for a client to make a correct assessment of the consequences of a release. The client, owing to a sense of loyalty, might not want or dare to say no to the therapist when asked for a release from confidentiality.

When the patient is a child, this matter comes to even more of a head. How can children assess the consequences of having the content of their therapy sessions spread to a wider audience? Can parents be considered to represent children in such tough situations?

These questions have been discussed intensively in recent years in connection with certain TV shows, where children have been interviewed. They have been exposed, fully recognizable, to TV audiences, in vulnerable situations, where therapists have also been involved. I belong to those who feel a profound unease about letting children be exposed in this way.

Elisabeth Cleve had cause to think long and hard about these ethical dilemmas, both on her own, and together with her colleagues, while she worked on the book that you now hold in your hands. She approached these questions with insight and humility. The viewpoints she put forth are important not only for this book's readers but also for anyone who might want to publish descriptions of troubled children and their reality in the future. Cleve was meticulous about giving an objective and accurate narrative of what happened in the therapy room while at the same time being careful to mask the child's identity. Only those closest to the children are meant to recognize who the children are. In addition, these adults, just as the children themselves, have received detailed information, including a chance to read and suggest changes in the manuscript, after which they have been positive toward the publication of the narratives.

The most important reason that people have been positive toward publication, I believe, is that Elisabeth Cleve describes her young patients in such a loving manner. She consistently underscores the positive aspects of the processes she depicts. The reader is both happy to meet these children and awed by them. What a strong spirit they show! And what imaginative survival strategies they come up with!

I wonder how the children will react when they read this book in fifteen or thirty years. My guess is that they are going to feel both restored and proud. Granted, the description of what has happened to them may not be something to include in their official curriculum vitae. But there is an inner CV that concerns how they became who they are. And in that CV, I believe these narratives will take a place of honour.

Lars H. Gustafsson
Paediatrician, Associate Professor of Social Medicine
Sweden

Foreword by Björn Salomonsson

Anyone who makes a discovery or has an important insight wants to tell the world about it. The scientist reports findings in a journal, the author writes a novel or a play, and the artist arranges an exhibition. For the psychotherapist, things are more complicated. Before reaching out to a larger readership she has to consider the issue of anonymity. Her patients must be certain that anything said or done in her office will remain undisclosed. So, how can she write about her work without transgressing these boundaries? She must also take into account the complexity of therapeutic work. Every event in a session may be viewed in relation to the previous session, the relationship with the therapist and the patient's life history. Each session is like a short story in a vast collection of such stories. To present such large and varied material and make good literature of it is a formidable task.

For the child therapist, two more problems emerge. One has to do with visualizing to adult readers the child's seemingly strange and alien world. Many of us have rather lopsided memories of our childhood. Some passionate drama, playful fantasy or ghastly horror may emerge in our memory now and then – but most childhood recollections lie embedded beneath a blanket of merciful oblivion. This can make it hard for any reader to understand a presentation of child therapy. The second problem has to do with yet another anonymity problem. A therapist who wishes to present adult therapy material asks the patient for permission. If the patient is a child this is not possible – at least not in the case of small children. The therapist must turn to the parents for permission, which poses an ethical challenge to both parties. What are we therapists to do if we wish to disseminate our experiences, insights and ideas about child psychotherapy? One solution is to publish case material in scientific journals, where only a limited number of professionals – whom we assume are aware of the ethical problems involved – will read it. But if we seek a larger audience, this solution will not work. Furthermore, such an audience will demand something more than a scientific presentation; they want good literature. For this audience the therapist must write in a fluent, respectful, empathic yet humorous style, touching both the reader's heart and intellect.

Few psychotherapists possess this gift. Elisabeth Cleve was one of these few. After taking her M.Sc. in psychology, she trained in the mid-1970s to become a child psychotherapist. This training took place at the Erica Foundation, an institution comparable to the Anna Freud Centre in London, with which it has long been engaged in a clinical and scientific exchange. She remained faithful to this institution until a malignant disease forced her to step back a few years before her retirement was due. She passed away in 2013.

Besides being an intuitive and sensitive psychotherapist, Elisabeth was a concrete and practical person with a firm footing in external reality. Early on, she realized the need for child psychotherapy to become more generally known. She therefore started to write books targeting a wider audience. In 2000, she published a lengthy account of a therapy with a boy diagnosed with a neuropsychiatric disorder. It was published by Karnac Books, London, in 2004 under the title *From Chaos to Coherence – Psychotherapy with a Little Boy with ADHD*. In 2002, she published her work with a two-and-a-half-year-old boy who had lost his mother and younger brother. It was also published by Karnac Books in 2008 under the title *A Big and a Little One Is Gone – Crisis Therapy with a Two-Year-Old Boy*.

The present book was published in Swedish in 2011. Elisabeth had a gift of capturing in a brief expression some piece of emotional reality. The original title testifies to that talent: *How Long Will She Be Dead?* These few words, seemingly so simple, bear witness to a child's despair. Ronia lost her mother at two years of age. Now she is seven years old and has many problems, not least with her schoolmates. The title's question reflects the double logic so common among children. Seven-year-old Ronia realizes that her mother is gone forever. Yet, "little" Ronia inside the "big" one maintains a secret bookkeeping in which mother will come back one day. The question is only "How long will she be dead?"

The stories about Ronia and the other children show not only Elisabeth's literary talent but also how she dealt with the issues of anonymity and ethics referred to earlier. I hope these stories will capture the reader's imagination and interest. They are poignant, humorous, moving, bewildering and intellectually stimulating; in short, they possess all the qualities that make for good reading. The honour of transferring these qualities from the Swedish original to English goes entirely to Pamela Boston. She is a translator who also cooperated with Elisabeth in connection with her two previous books published in English.

Björn Salomonsson
M.D., Ph. D., Child Psychoanalyst (IPA)
Department of Women's and Children's Health
Karolinska Institutet
Stockholm, Sweden

Author's preface

I have had a long career as a psychologist and psychotherapist for children and adolescents at the Erica Foundation in Stockholm, Sweden. This work has meant many meetings with children with severe difficulties. Some of them have come for a psychological assessment in order to shed light on the causes of their suffering, while others have participated in short-term therapy after a traumatic experience that has afflicted them and their family. Sometimes I have only needed to carry out supportive talks with worried parents. I have also been a supervisor for colleagues both from the Erica Foundation and from other clinics working with children in crisis and chaos.

In this book I share my experiences and show how children with psychic problems can get help to go forward with their lives. I describe how Ali comes in for a psychological assessment even though he does not want to be assessed. It is only his mother who wants it. Malte goes to crisis therapy after a sexual assault. Ronia goes through a short-term crisis therapy several years after her mother's death. Olga's psychologist receives supervision from me in order to gain a better understanding of her patient.

The narratives about these four children rest entirely upon my personal clinical documentation. The psychological processes are described exactly as they have taken place. Aside from certain information about the families that would have made it possible to identify them, nothing has been altered to any essential degree. The reader gets a chance to follow each child's pathway toward a better psychic well-being from three perspectives: mine, the child's and the parents'. My hope is that the book will convey knowledge about the life force that children possess inside, even in times of great distress. I want to show that when they receive help, there is always hope for the better.

I would like to express my heartfelt gratitude to Malte, Ronia, Olga and Ali. They have let me witness their unconquerable spirits as they have struggled to regain their sense of well-being. I also extend my special thanks to their parents, who so generously have given me their consent to write this book. Thanks go as well to Olga's psychologist – whom I will, for reasons of anonymity, merely call Jenny – for letting me tell about the supervision I gave her.

To write authentic narratives about child patients is a balancing act that calls for considerable reflection. I therefore gratefully acknowledge the positive support and creative encouragement that I have received from all of my present and former colleagues at the Erica Foundation and from psychotherapists Britta Blomberg, May Nilsson, Anita Dahlgren, Ewa Heller Ekblad and Willemo Nilsson, for their constructive review of the manuscript.

I would like to thank Associate Professor Gunnar Carlberg, director of the Erica Foundation, both for encouraging me to write about my work and for thoroughly reviewing the manuscript. I also thank him for many years of good collaboration at the Erica Foundation. Warm thanks go as well to Magnus Kihlbom, the former chief psychiatrist at the Erica Foundation, for his encouragement and constructive viewpoints on the content of the book.

Special thanks go to the following people who have reviewed the chapters dealing with themes within their areas of expertise: psychotherapists Miriam Alvebäck and Bengt Söderström, who have broad experience of work with sexually assaulted children, and Associate Professor Marie-Louise Ögren at the University of Stockholm, who has special expertise on supervision.

I greatly appreciate the care and energy that Pamela Boston has put into the translation of this book.

I thank the Vårstavi Foundation and the Erica Foundation for their grants, making it possible for me to reduce my working hours and compile material for my book.

I would also like to thank my family: my daughters, Susanna and Catharina, for their unflagging interest in my work, and my husband, Egon, for his patience and helpfulness with practical tasks connected to the book.

Finally, I would like to extend especially heartfelt words of thanks to Anna and Coco Belfrage, Arild, Sweden, and their family. Their commitment and generous economic support have made it possible for me to write this book. Their contribution has come from donations to the foundation that the family set up to honour the memory of their daughter Tove Belfrage, who died in a traffic accident in the summer of 2008. She left behind a husband and a one-year-old daughter, as well as other dearly beloved family members.

The family's wish has been that donations to their foundation should be used to spread knowledge about how we can help children who have experienced a severe trauma to go forward and have a good life. I hope that this book, which I have been entrusted to write, will come to serve such a purpose.

Stockholm, spring 2012
Elisabeth Cleve

Introduction

The child psychologist meets the children

In this book readers are given a chance to follow my work with four of my young patients – Malte, Ronia, Olga and Ali. All of them have experienced severe traumas, which have left them with deep psychic wounds. Their suffering manifests itself through various psychic symptoms. Regardless of the different nature of their traumas and of their reactions, they have one thing in common. All of them have an inner life force that makes it possible for them to go forward with their lives. When I work with these children, my aim is to help them to discover their life force for themselves. After the conclusion of therapy they can continue to rely on their newly found strength and thus feel more at peace with themselves and with life.

The target groups for my books are child care professionals and anyone else who works with children, as well as parents and the general public. Both those who already have a great deal of knowledge and those who have a general interest will find much food for thought in my narratives. Children are different and the psychological help needed by each individual one of them has been adapted thereafter. Three of the children are advised to go to crisis therapy, which is a type of time-limited short-term therapy. In the text I use the two concepts interchangeably. In one of the cases I also describe the supervision received at the same time by the psychologist who is conducting therapy with the child. The fourth and last presentation concerns a boy who undergoes psychological assessment in order to shed light on the causes of his symptoms.

In the first chapter "Grown-Ups Mustn't Do Stuff like That to Little Kids, . . . Right?" I describe how the mother of a boy named Malte, five years old, calls and asks for help for her son, who has "gone through something horrible". He has been sexually assaulted. The family is in shock and the parents are unable to cope with the situation. The boy is silent, the mum is devastated and cries, while the dad is angry and threatens to go after the perpetrator.

Malte begins a crisis therapy that consists of twelve sessions, while the parents are offered support discussions. The work is described session for session for both Malte and his parents. A special aspect of Malte's therapy is that he gets a chance to make and illustrate a little book about what happened to him. His advanced computer skills serve him well in the production of the book. This is his way of using therapy to work through a horrible experience.

In Chapter 2, "How Long Will She Be Dead?", we meet a father who has an urgent need to get help for his daughter. In the chapter I tell about Ronia, who is seven years old. Her mother died when she was two years old. Difficulties have existed the entire time but everything seemed to be going in the right direction until recently. Ronia is showing anxiety symptoms as never before. Over a short period of time she has been faced with many changes in her life. She, her sister and her dad have moved into a new flat with dad's new partner and her three sons. Added to that, she has to cope with a new school start. Ronia feels alone and different. "Everyone else has a mother," she laments, and the people around her cannot stop feeling sorry for her.

Ronia starts a crisis therapy of ten sessions on the condition that she will not have to listen to "busybody talk". She stages her sense of loss toward her mother through the things she eagerly builds in the sand tray and her games with the dolls that live in the dollhouse. Toward the end of therapy Ronia dares to ask, "How long will she be dead?" She receives a heavy-hearted but honest answer from me. Now she can finally stop waiting for her mother to come back and instead look forward. After therapy she presents herself to others as a schoolgirl and not as a poor, pitiful little motherless thing.

Chapter 3 tells of two loving adoptive parents who are extremely worried about their daughter Olga, ten years old. She is in low spirits, has serious concentration problems and cannot keep up with her schoolwork. She becomes terror-stricken when faced with leave-taking, short as well as long. She also thinks that everything about her is wrong. She sees herself as a second-rate girl surrounded by people who are equally second-rate. In her time-limited short-term therapy with her psychologist, Jenny, Olga is helped to understand her own part in making her schoolmates not want to play with her. She also ceases seeing people, including herself, as defective and second-rate.

The chapter about Olga is called "Children Who Feel Second-Rate Make Others Feel the Same Way". It is written from my perspective as supervisor for Olga's psychologist Jenny. The narrative is based on sequences from Olga's therapy that Jenny describes for me. These descriptions are often tied to questions that Jenny initiates during our four supervision meetings. Jenny's need to understand Olga gives rise to many stimulating exchanges between us. Olga makes her psychologist feel second-rate in the same way as she herself feels. It is painful for Jenny to be unable to help the child who needs her help so badly. The reader gets a chance to follow how the psychologist avails herself of supervision in order to work through the feelings that are evoked in therapy with this unhappy child. Jenny finds her way out of the strong psychological force field in which Olga has unconsciously trapped her. As a result, Olga becomes able to accept help from Jenny.

In Chapter 4 we meet Ali. Like Ronia he is seven years old and is in his first year of school. His teacher urges his mother to contact a child psychologist to get help for her son. Ali is violent in school and it is hard to communicate with him. He attacks other children, says that he is going to kill himself, gives people the finger and hisses "fuck you" to the teachers. Ali was born in Sweden but his single mother has fled here from traumatic experiences in war-torn Iraq. The chapter "A Mother's Trauma Becomes Her Son's Trauma" gives an account of the psychological assessment that Ali undergoes with me. He makes four visits but refuses to carry out the test tasks that children usually enjoy. My sessions with Ali are both sweaty and loud. He screams at the top of his lungs, "Help, help! She's hitting me!" But when he understands that such tricks do not work, he starts to participate in his own way.

A challenging and exciting cooperation develops, which shows how underlying causes affect his present disturbed and disturbing behaviour. After twelve years Ali and I happen to meet, to our mutually pleasant surprise. He has turned into a handsome young man of nineteen years who has just graduated from upper secondary school. During a long discussion at a café, he tells me about his life.

What he remembers of the psychological assessment is that it "opened mum's eyes" and that she in her turn was able to open his eyes so that he understood which paths he should choose.

In the penultimate chapter, "Sharing Narratives about Child Patients –: Is That Acceptable?", I bring up ethical considerations and also give practical advice on what to remember when preparing for the publication of confidentiality-classified patient material. I also describe how formerly confidentiality-classified material should be handled, meaning after the families have given their written permission that the material may be published. The parents of Malte, Ronia, Olga and Ali have all signed release contracts. Jenny and I, on the other hand, have simply made a spoken agreement.

1 Grown-ups mustn't do stuff like that to little kids, . . . right?

Malte, five years old, comes to crisis therapy after a sexual assault

Police unable to establish that a crime has been committed

One day in November, just before our telephone contact hours are over, we get a call from a mother whose voice is heavy with sadness. She says that she needs help for her five-year-old son who has "gone through something horrible". The psychologist who answers the call asks her to say what has happened. It turns out that her son has been sexually assaulted. The incident came to light a week ago but actually took place during the summer. The mother says that the family is in shock and cannot cope with the situation. When she is asked whether they have reported the incident to the police, she answers that her husband has done so but that they have not heard anything back. The psychologist asks if the parents want to come in for a talk. The mother immediately replies in the affirmative. When she notices that it is taking a little time for the psychologist to find an opening, she hastens to say that she and her husband can come at any time whatsoever.

I am entrusted with the case, and the parents come to see me for a one-hour talk a couple of days later. They are in their forties and look both distraught and needy as they hurry into the room. When we shake hands and greet each other, I notice that the mother's hand is shaking. Their names are Annika and Jonathan and their son's name is Malte. When the discussion gets under way, they speak at the same time. They feel an urgency to recount everything as carefully as possible. Their narrative alternates between emotional outbursts and facts. Sometimes in the course of our talk they do not keep to chronological order, which does not exactly make it easy for me to follow their story. Therefore, I stop them every now and then and ask for clarification. This is what they tell me.

Last summer, during the first two weeks of the school's summer holiday, they had employed Jack, a young man in his twenties, as a babysitter for their three children. This was before the parents' holiday had started. They always have to make this kind of arrangement since their children have more time off than they do. Besides Malte, who has had his fifth birthday this autumn, they have two older children, two daughters – Linda, ten years old, and Johanna, twelve years old.

They were often over at their friends' houses when Jack was working for their family. Malte and Jack were thus often left alone together.

A neighbour of the family, Iris, had recommended Jack because he was "so sweet and helpful and good with children". She herself had used him as a babysitter for her two preschool-age daughters. Neither Iris nor Annika and Jonathan had sensed that anything was wrong. Quite the opposite. They had considered Jack to be an open and pleasant young man and had taken an immediate liking to him. The children had also liked him. They had gone swimming, and Jack had worked with Malte on his strokes and kicks since Malte could not yet swim. Jack had played the guitar and had sung with the children. He had fixed a flat tire on one of the girls' bicycles. Malte had been especially impressed that Jack could talk like Donald Duck. Jack was going to teachers' college. Annika, who is a teacher herself, had enjoyed hearing about his studies. After two weeks, Jack had ended his work with them according to plan, and the family went away on a holiday trip. Annika and Jonathan had been pleased with the summer, the nice weather and their seemingly contented children.

Malte has changed as the autumn has progressed. He can no longer sleep in his room but instead comes to his parents' bed. He has also started to wet the bed at night. He has nightmares and mumbles in his sleep about someone who might come and get him. He is pale and listless and has been unable to say if anything is bothering him. When they have asked if anything hurts, he has sometimes put his hand on his stomach. Annika has taken Malte to the doctor but all the tests have come back negative and the doctor could not find anything wrong with his stomach. Jonathan talked to the preschool teachers a month ago and they had also observed that Malte was not his usual happy and creative self. They had believed that he was unhappy because one of his playmates wanted to play with another boy. Malte tires easily at preschool, and the teachers have wondered if he is on the verge of some illness. He is well liked by the other children for his curiosity and stamina, but now he does not feel like playing.

Two weeks ago Annika and Jonathan found out the reason behind Malte's unhappiness. Annika was watching the news on TV when Malte came to her and started to talk about the summer. She had asked him if he missed Jack. To her astonishment Malte had answered emphatically that he did not. She thought that sounded strange and asked him how he could say such a thing. He was nasty, Malte answered. Annika had protested and said that all three children had been fond of Jack. Malte held his ground and said curtly, "Jack was nasty even though he was nice." Annika sensed something awful, turned off the TV and told Malte that they had to get to the bottom of this. It finally came out that Jack had pulled and jerked his own penis and "bothered" Malte's penis so that it had hurt. Malte also said, "He didn't say he was sorry even though he hurt me. He really didn't say he was sorry, mum." When Annika had asked why Malte had not told her about this earlier, he said between sobs, "I wasn't allowed to." At this point the conversation came to an end. Malte cried and Annika, in shock, called for Jonathan, who came to their side right away.

When Malte's parents have come thus far in their narrative, I can see that they are shocked, miserable and devastated. They express their feelings in their own ways.

Annika cries and wipes away her tears, but she cannot stop crying. Jonathan swears and shouts in desperation that he wants to "wring that creep's neck". He also says, "Our entire existence has been turned upside down. Everything we've built up has plunged into chaos." Jonathan also has tears in his eyes and must blow his nose before he continues talking. He says that Malte has become withdrawn and does not want to say anything more about what happened, at least not to his dad. They have not asked the doctor to examine Malte since so much time has passed.

Based on their narrative, I summarize my impressions and say it seems that Malte is not the only one who needs help. His parents could use some as well. They say nothing but just look as though they have been drained of all energy. They look at each other and while Annika blows her nose, Jonathan finally answers yes for both of them and asks what they can do. Before we continue I want to know if the police have scheduled an interview with Malte and, if so, when it is going to be. Annika and Jonathan know nothing about this but say they will check with the police right away. When they submitted the report of misconduct, they were told that it would take a few weeks before anything more would happen. We conclude our talk by agreeing that they will contact me as soon as the police interview has been conducted. At that point I want to meet Malte together with his mum and dad and see how he feels. After that, if I find he needs professional help, I plan to suggest how such help could best be set up, also including them. Annika and Jonathan think this approach sounds good.

Meeting with Malte and his parents

Three weeks later I meet Malte with his mum and dad. I want to gain an understanding of Malte's psychic condition in order to determine whether he needs crisis therapy. I already know that his parents are distraught. When they come into my room Malte looks around cautiously and then sits down close to his mum, who has seated herself on the couch, while his dad has chosen the armchair beside it. Malte fools around with a rubber band and some paper clips that he has in the pocket of his jeans. He is a pale, tall five-year-old with some adorable freckles and greyish-blue eyes that take a quick look in the direction where I am sitting. He has eczema on his wrists and neck, and he has scratched at it so much that he has made it bleed.

I start out by asking Annika and Jonathan if they have talked to Malte about why they are coming to see me. They nod in the affirmative. It is important for Malte to know what I know, since the reason for the visit is so sensitive. I describe briefly for Malte my knowledge about what has happened to him and inform him that I have learned this from his parents. I say that Jack has treated Malte in a wrong and nasty way and that grown-ups are not allowed to do to children what Jack did. I then go over to making small talk for a little while, and I note that Malte is listening even though he is not looking in my direction. He says nothing.

Annika says that the police interview has taken place and that the next step, a preliminary investigation, has been dismissed. I am not surprised to hear this. Suspicions of sexual assault on children seldom lead to legal action. It is considered more or less impossible to prove that a crime has been committed. Jack has denied everything, so it is a matter of word against word. Annika was present at the interview. She thought that Malte would say more if she was there and not Jonathan, since he, in her words, cannot control himself. Jonathan is outraged and says:

A little kid is apparently chanceless against an adult, against a creep like that! It's too bloody awful!

Annika shushes Jonathan and I continue talking to Malte:

I'm not a policewoman who interviews children when a grown-up has done something bad to them. I'm someone who helps children and their mums and dads so that everything will be good again. I usually do that. Children come to see me every day with their parents.

I ask Annika and Malte to tell me about the interview. Malte indicates that he does not want to talk. He stares at the toy cupboard, so I say to him:

It's fine for you to go over there and play. You can still listen to what we are talking about.

Annika says that the interviewing officer was a policewoman who had neither a gun nor a uniform. Malte had expected to get to see a police car. When they were back at home he told his mum that she should have asked if the policewoman had caught any bad guys. Malte was disappointed that all she had were dolls and "she asked so much about loads of stuff". Annika says that the interview was not easy for Malte. He had done his best to answer the questions while the officer repeated them over and over again. He thought all this repetition meant that he had given the wrong answer. Now Malte partakes actively but wordlessly in our discussion and looks like he approves of the way his mum is recounting what happened.

After hearing about the interview I want to hear how the family is doing now, and I toss out the question to whoever wants to answer it. Jonathan does not want to embarrass Malte, so he asks his son to stop him if he says something wrong. Turned toward Malte, who goes on moving the trains and cars around in the sand tray, Jonathan begins:

You're unhappy and you don't feel like playing. You don't even want to ride your bike, something you're so good at. You don't want to sleep in your own bed. As we all know, you're usually a happy kid who loves preschool.

Malte leans a little farther over the sand tray but does not seem to mind if his dad continues, and so he does:

When you were a little baby you had eczema, and it's come back. You often complain about how it itches so badly and stings when we put ointment on it. So we put it on at night after you've gone to sleep because then it doesn't hurt.

The atmosphere in the room is calm. Malte does not respond and Annika goes over and sits down beside him, pats him on the head and fills in:

And you don't like pasta with ketchup any more. You always used to love it.

After a short pause she adds:

Dad and I don't want you to be unhappy. And you wet the bed at night. That's okay, but you stopped doing that a long, long time ago, several years ago.

It is completely silent in the room. Malte feels uncomfortable about what Annika just said. It seems as though he sees wetting the bed as incredibly babyish and embarrassing.

The silence remains and after a while I break it:

Children can do that sometimes, even though they don't want to. That happens to many children. It can happen even when someone is so big that he stopped wetting his bed long ago. This is especially true when someone is not feeling good. It stops when he is feeling better again.

I round off the meeting by turning to Malte and saying:

Your parents want everything to be good for you again, yes, for the whole family. You and your mum and dad may come to see me more times. Children who come here get to play and build with the things in the sand tray. And we usually do some other stuff, too, like drawing, colouring and writing. How do you think that sounds?

Malte does not answer, so Annika asks:

Do you want to come here again and see Elisabeth and build in her sand tray? I can tell you that dad and I really want to come here.

Malte, who wants to stop wetting the bed, gives me a quick glance and answers almost in a whisper:

Maybe I do, but maybe just a little.

I continue to tell him:

Mums and dads get help here, too. They usually want to talk. Children don't have to talk if they don't feel like it. It's up to them. Your whole family is going to feel better after you've come here a few times – your sisters, too.

We have not had time to talk so much about the daughters at this meeting, but the parents have talked to them and are convinced that Jack did not do anything inappropriate to them. Nevertheless, I assume that what has happened to Malte has affected them as well. Perhaps they feel guilty for not having noticed what was happening to their little brother. Maybe they preferred to be with their friends and did not want Malte to disturb them when Jack was around. I sense that Malte is gazing at my back when I turn away from him. He is listening to my words but saying nothing. He just goes on driving the cars around in the sand tray. He likes trains, boats and cars, but also shows interest in my soldiers, cowboys and Indians while at the same time not removing them from the toy cupboard.

His dad, who wants Malte to come out with a more definite answer, asks:

Do you want to come back to see Elisabeth?

Malte nods in assent and I say:

Okay then, it's decided. I also want to see you, Malte, very much.

Afterwards, Malte is the first to extend his hand to mine when we say goodbye. I keep his hand in my grip for a moment and give it a little squeeze. Malte responds with the hint of a smile before he darts away. His parents get the times and dates for the coming visits.

Symptoms after the trauma

My impression after having met Malte with his mum and dad is that all three of them need help. Jonathan clinches his jaw and must strain himself to stay calm and not raise his voice too much during our talk. Judging from Annika's way of relating to him, I guess that Jonathan on some occasion has lost control of himself at home, bawled people out and shouted lots of things in sheer desperation. He gets a look from his wife from time to time that prompts him to hold his temper. He has also noticed himself that Malte gets a cautious look on his face when he glances at his dad.

I believe that Malte is a cheerful boy under normal circumstances who now has lost his sense of psychic well-being. He has previously trusted in the future and has yearned to be big enough to start school, Annika says. Now he no longer mentions school. His sisters have taught him to write some of the letters of the alphabet. I heard him talking to his parents in the waiting room and noted his good vocabulary, which makes me believe that he is a talkative boy under normal circumstances. Now he is dejected and in low spirits but brightens up when I say that I usually help children and their mums and dads. He is also curious about the toys that I have in the room.

Malte most certainly has never had his trust betrayed by an adult before. His parents watch over him with loving care and are deeply concerned about his well-being. But now he has been betrayed and disappointed in one of the most horrible ways possible. He liked Jack in the beginning and looked up to him. Jack knew how to do so many things and was so helpful. Then without warning Jack turned out to be ruthless, completely lacking in respect. He was anything but sweet and helpful. He crushed Malte's will and violated him sexually. Malte has found himself in a vulnerable position where he has not been able to protect himself or his body. Prior to this assault, he has not even been aware that he would ever need to defend himself against such a thing.

Annika's impression from her talks with Malte about the assault is that he is confused and does not fully understand what has happened to him. It is common that children who have been violated experience feelings of unreality in the same way as Malte does. A child's way of withstanding an assault is to block off sensory impressions and repress frightening memory images. As a result, children cannot always talk about what they have experienced in a credible way. Malte is also unsure about who was at fault. Perhaps he thinks that the fault, partly or fully, is his. In addition, Jack has ordered him not to tell anyone anything. He shows in his nightmares that he is also afraid that someone is going to come after him.

Malte is also bewildered over his parents' strong reactions and terrified about being the cause of this emotional tumult. As he perceives things, it most likely seems that he is the source of his mum's unhappiness and his dad's fury. Perhaps he also believes that his dad is angry at him and not at Jack. Malte is too young to understand causal relationships. In order to give Malte a chance to work through his trauma, which is also his parents' trauma, I propose a twelve-session crisis therapy for Malte. This is a form of time-limited short-term therapy – one session per week, and forty-five minutes per session. His parents will get some supportive talks during the same time period as Malte has his therapy.

My purpose with therapy for Malte is to give him an opportunity to work through his memories and reactions after the assault. He needs help in approaching, one step at a time, the confusing memories, the mixed-up feelings and the chaotic reactions that resulted when the assault came to light. For Malte causal relationships are all jumbled up, and he does not understand why he has broken out in such an irritating rash on his neck or why he has lost all his energy. He cannot communicate what he has experienced but instead contains the chaos inside himself.

Malte needs to find better ways to express his anxiety and distress than through nightmares, wetting the bed and breaking out in eczema. When therapy begins, Malte will get a chance to express what has happened on a symbolic level through games and play. He will get a chance to choose what he wants to play with. The basis for a good working atmosphere between the two of us will also be laid during this time. He needs to see that he can confide in me and that I will respect his confidences and treat them discreetly. This is a precondition for the development of our therapeutic work. The goal is for him, when therapy is over, to be able to think about and talk about the incident without feeling bad.

When Malte can put into words what he is feeling and thinking, it will be also easier for his parents to understand when he needs their comfort and support. An important ingredient of the therapy will also be to make clear what is right versus what is wrong in relationships between children and grown-ups. Malte needs to hear this from more adults, not just his mum and dad. Finally, our work in therapy will help him to find his way back to the boy he was before, cheerful and full of ideas, the Malte who loves to play and ride bikes with his playmates at preschool.

The focus in my discussions with Malte's parents will be to help them relate emotionally to what has happened and to respect each other's ways of expressing their feelings. When they get into a row because of their different temperaments, neither Malte nor they themselves can benefit; quite the opposite. His mum's tears and his dad's anger have their origins in the same despair. They have to get through this together. They gratefully accept my proposal to help them because there is nothing they want more than for the family to get into balance again. They also have many questions, for example, whether all of this can affect Malte as a grown man.

In the therapy with Malte I will approach the assault more directly after a certain amount of time. I am also going to avail myself of a psychological tool called *Book about What Happened.* A colleague of mine, psychologist Bengt Söderström, has devised this tool. He has extensive experience of work with sexually traumatized children at one of the special treatment centres in Stockholm. My idea is to make a little book of this type together with Malte. We will approach what happened in many different ways, depending on what Malte chooses, but the book will be an important element. I am going to start with it when he is ready. I will follow his pace and momentum.

The whole process must take place in small steps since Malte at this point in time does not want to think about what has happened. In any event, the book provides a gentle way of approaching difficult issues. The book will be plain and simple and will consist of ten pages, with a drawing of one figure or more and a couple of sentences on each page. Malte will be the main character in the book. Each page will highlight a certain part of what happened, all in chronological order. In this way the course of events will be moved forward until the point at which the entire incident has been described in words and pictures. The story will start before the assault and will end with positive thoughts about facing the future.

I think out the general contours of the textual content in advance. In contrast, the pictures will evolve as we go along. Time will tell how and when we can start with the book. It is important for Malte to feel that I respect his wishes regardless of whether he wants to work with the book. He has been subjected to actions where his "no" has not been respected. He has had his trust betrayed by a person he has trusted and liked. When things like this happen, it is hard for a child to sort out his negative and positive feelings. I will do my best to listen well when I am in the presence of Malte and to be on the lookout for what he wants to stage in his play.

In this narrative about the healing process that Malte goes through, I choose to focus on our work making the *Book about What Happened.* When a child in therapy is not more than five years old, we can count on many other things to happen that also help to move the process forward. Selected vignettes that illustrate such factors are also included but I have had to omit many examples. In short, Malte comes to see me twelve times, Tuesdays at 11.00 a.m., and every session is forty-five minutes long. My talks with his parents are also described.

Crisis therapy with twelve sessions

Sessions 1–3

Malte shows from the beginning that he is worried about being alone in the room with me. His dad accompanies him to the first session and sits on a chair outside my room. I do not close the door but Malte closes it himself during the second session. In the introductory phase I let Malte take in the atmosphere of the room. How does it feel for him to be alone with me? Despite all efforts to put him at ease, maybe he thinks our meetings are going to resemble the police interview. Or maybe he does not expect another such experience but is still wary that we are going to spend most of the time *talking* about what happened. Anything connected to the assault is painful for Malte to think about. At the police station he talked because he had to. After that he has not mentioned anything about the theme at home. I hope that he will gradually feel that he can trust me.

I tell him once more that my name is Elisabeth, and his whispered answer is barely audible:

I know.

That he remembers my name probably means that his parents have prepared him for the sessions. I have told him earlier but I tell him again what children get a chance to do when they come to see me.

You're not going to need to answer loads of questions. You've already done that at the police station. No, here you get to look around and see what you want to do.

Malte stands just inside the door and looks hesitant so I continue:

You can paint, colour, play games, build things in the sand tray, check out the dollhouse, or do anything else that you feel like doing. Talking about different things, well, that's something we can do later if you feel like it.

When Malte is alone with me, he is like most children inasmuch as he picks up more of what I say than he does when his parents are present. He most likely let his parents listen on his account when we met the previous time. He looks as though he is hearing for the first time that he can use the toys in the room, draw, paint, colour or build in the sand tray. I have laid out crayons, paper, pens and paints, since I have the work with the book in mind. We will need the material when that time comes. It instils a sense of security in therapy if the room looks the same every time. The same material is laid out for every visit, even if Malte does not use it.

I tell him a little about other children who come to see me:

Many children come here who are having a hard time with different things, or who are unhappy about something that has happened.

I mention some reasons for coming that are similar to Malte's own problems:

Some have stomach aches, others have no friends, some wet their beds even though they don't want to. Others have a hard time sleeping in their own beds, and some are unhappy.

Malte listens while I talk about the other children, and I notice a twitching in the corner of his mouth when I mention children who wet their beds.

Here in therapy all these children get help so that things get better again. I want to help you feel good again as well.

In the first session Malte ventures a cautious glance at the paper for painting. I reach out to him with a piece of paper and say:

If you want to, you can draw your family when all of you are doing something.
Well, okay, Malte says quietly.

With some hesitation he begins to draw. He holds the pencil as a younger child would and draws a shaky head-foot man, a head with legs and arms attached to it. After a short while I ask him:

Who is that? Who have you drawn?
I want to write my letters.

He writes "MALTE" over the entire figure, and with that he considers the task completed. I ask where the rest of the family is, but he stands firm:

It's me. There's no room for the others. I don't want to draw 'cause it's no fun. And besides I never drawed a girl in my whole life.

I see from his picture that he is not used to drawing, but perhaps he also lacks the psychic energy to think about the rest of his family after all the turbulence that has arisen.

Malte remains seated, and I tell him to feel free to take a look around the room. He slides down from the chair and glides around the room, checking out the games and toys and getting a feel of the sand in the sand tray. He fiddles with a few cowboys and Indians. He checks out the cars and comments to himself about their makes. He is eager to see what is behind or under other things in the room. He opens a closet door and takes a peek into the closet, looks under a radiator and behind a picture that is hanging on the wall. He looks at me for permission when he wants to open a desk drawer and I give a yes signal. Perhaps Malte is making sure that there is nothing dangerous there. He is sombre but still gives an impression of being curious and eager to learn.

He needs the first three sessions to become less anxious and to start liking to come see me. He plays in the sand tray most of the time. He looks up at me now and then, while he talks out loud to himself. In that way he lets me go along with him in his games. What Malte likes best is to set up different teams that fight against each other. The teams consist of tame and wild animals as well as soldiers, cowboys and Indians. The team formations vary; sometimes they are equal in strength, but often a "little and weak and nice" team fights against a "strong and nasty" one. The figures suddenly change sides and the game becomes agitated. In the next battle the figures that have previously been nice can become nasty. I see how he tries to solve situations like this by moving the figures around again. This makes things even more confusing, with Indians and cowboys who now stand in disarray and shoot their own team players in the back. Malte cannot figure out how to put things in order again in these battles so he ends the game abruptly.

Malte does what most children usually do at the beginning of therapy. He stages in his games what has happened to him. For him, chaos takes over when "weak" must fight against "strong". He himself has not been able to cope with such a situation and neither can his animals or warriors. It does not matter whether the figures belong to the "nasty" or the "nice" team; the chaos is the same. I see this as Malte's way of expressing his own confusion after what has happened to him, which he must do before we go further. During these first three sessions Malte does not even look at the crayons, paints, pencils, paintbrushes or paper. He has now started to show his interest in me by not only taking a peek at me but also by looking me straight in the eye. He talks less to himself and more to me. I see a hint of a smile from time to time. Otherwise he is occupied with cowboys, Indians and warriors who keep shooting indiscriminately.

Mum cries and dad is furious

Discussion with Malte's parents

After Malte has had three sessions, his parents come in for a talk. Malte's dad can get away from his job more easily than his mum, so he is the one who will usually bring Malte to therapy. I tell Annika and Jonathan that Malte is feeling his way around in therapy. His mum thinks I mean that he is not making progress and asks anxiously:

What are we going to do if he doesn't get happy and well again?

The most important thing here and now is to instil hope in Malte's parents. I therefore refer to my many years of experience of good results from this type of treatment, and I add that this holds true for both children and their parents.

They smile and look less worried. Before I let them talk I want to clarify:

At this point Malte is still in the beginning of his therapy, and we must allow the process to take time. Therapy is divided into three different phases, and as time goes on, changes are going to take place. Your son is not slower than other children.

My words have a calming effect on Jonathan, who is eager for a chance to start talking. He is still upset and says:

My son's been violated and I'm suffering with him. He's changed from a happy little kid to a silent and tormented soul. I just can't stand it.

Jonathan drowns out both Annika and me. He gets annoyed at his wife, who shushes him and does not want him to talk so loudly. I also say that it would be a good idea for him to speak a little more quietly because then I can understand what he is saying more easily. At this point he asks me:

How would you react if your own child had been attacked by such a creep and then was not believed?

I would react exactly as you two are doing, with despair, with frustration at my powerlessness and anger.

I think this feeling of powerlessness is the worst. I am SO damned mad.

I agree:

I would feel that way, too, SO damned mad. No doubt whatsoever.

I have a warm feeling for Malte's parents. They are in despair and have a hard time talking to each other about what has happened, and my suggestion before we go on is as follows:

I want to divide the time equally between you two today, so that both of you get a chance to tell me how you're feeling and thinking.

Jonathan gets to start in order to ease the pressure inside him. In his anxiety-ridden state he does not have the presence of mind for a dialogue just now.

Then I want to hear how you, Annika, experience the situation, I say.

She answers:

Jonathan can talk as long as he wants to because it makes me feel better if he calms down.

However, I stand firm and clear:

No, both of you must get a chance to express your frustration and listen to the other's feelings and reactions. You need help, all three of you.

The mood in the room becomes calmer and Jonathan begins:

Everything has turned into chaos in my head, and at home it's the same thing. I get angry about everything and lose my temper. I've phoned my job and said that I'm ill. I can't think straight. They asked what my illness was, and I said I damned well didn't know what my illness was but I know I'm ill.

It becomes clear that what weighs on Jonathan's mind most heavily is his not having been able to protect his family. He loses his temper with his daughters, too. One time he blamed them for not noticing anything strange about that creep Jack. He had immediately regretted his words, but it was too late to take them back. Both daughters had started crying. They slipped into the one girl's room and stayed there the entire evening.

They don't go over to their friends' houses and they don't talk on their cell phones any more. I miss that chitchat that can drive me crazy under normal circumstances, says Jonathan and looks devastated.

When his time is almost up, he says:

Can kids get a warped view toward sex when they grow up because of stuff like this? I mean we see stories about perverts who become perpetrators, about how they were violated themselves when they were kids.

My answer is this:

Those perpetrators have not had parents who gave them loving care. Malte has such parents to the greatest degree. Besides, he goes to therapy and that's going to help him, both in the short and the long term.

We talk about this issue for a while, until I say that it is Annika's turn to speak. Jonathan leans back in the armchair, blows his nose and is obviously in a state of intense emotion. Annika has her handkerchief ready when she starts to speak:

I feel awful all the time and cry over nothing. Everything's so hard. We don't do anything fun in the family. No one has the energy. A neighbour rang our doorbell and asked if something had happened to us, and I told her to go home and mind her own business. I mean, that's crazy. She just wanted to help and she had no idea what was going on. I feel so sorry for the kids, too. They don't feel like doing anything any more.

When Annika talks about the children she cries for a long while, and Jonathan's glasses are misty as he lays his hand on his wife's shoulder. When she regains her composure she continues:

It's so hard when everything falls on my shoulders. And I'm also scared to death all the time.

When I ask her what she is most scared of, she turns to her husband and says:

That you're going to do something you'll regret.

Jonathan knows what his wife is referring to and responds:

Yes, okay, okay, I've said I'm going to go after that creep and give him what he deserves. I was SO damned mad. I don't know what I'm going to do.

I ask Jonathan:

Have you become afraid of yourself and all the feelings that have been awakened in you now that someone has violated your child?

Jonathan replies:

I've never felt like this before.

I concur:

This is one of the worst things that a parent can experience, that someone hurts his child. It arouses lots of primitive feelings. But, of course, there's a difference between thinking about something and actually doing it.

Jonathan nods in agreement.

Do you have thoughts like that now, thoughts that you want to go after Jack? It's important for Annika to know.

He looks at her and says:

You needn't be afraid. I'm not going to do that. I promise. Anyhow I can't do anything because all of my energy's gone. I can't even do my job, you know.

The best way you can use any energy you might have left is to make sure you're able to come here. You're going to feel better if you do.

Yes, we've put your schedule paper up on our fridge, Annika comments.

When they stand up to go, they seem less burdened. Annika has stopped crying and runs her hand quickly over the nape of Jonathan's neck. The most important task for this meeting has been to help Annika and Jonathan listen to each other and respect the fact that they express their feelings in different ways.

Book about What Happened

Session 4

When we have reached this point, Malte is used to coming to see me and he feels more secure. He runs up to my room on his own every time. His dad or his maternal grandmother brings him here and waits in the waiting room. Malte has now had his fill of the messy battles in the sand tray and looks around in the room to see what he wants to do instead. At this point I suggest that the two of us together can start making a book with drawings and texts, a book about what happened. I take a pencil and some paper and get ready to start drawing. But Malte insists:

I don't like to draw. It's no fun. I almost never draw.

I try with:

Let's do it together. Come and let me show you.

Malte responds by getting keyed up, twisting and turning around on the floor, scampering randomly about in the room, looking out the window and talking about something he sees down below on the street. He chuckles in a way to divert me, to get me to stop talking about "that thing" that he does not want to talk about. He lets me sit alone at the table with my blank paper. I use a pencil and draw a boy. He asks me as he chuckles:

And what's that thing s'posed to be?

I answer with a counter-question in an attempt to capture his interest:

What do you think it looks like?

Malte shakes his head in the negative.

A boy who's riding a bike, I say.
Well, I never coulda' guessed it.

I chuckle at his frankness. He also laughs. Like Malte, I do not get a lot of practice at drawing.

He goes to the shelf where I have the cars and checks out all the car makes. When he stretches in order to take down some aeroplanes from the top shelf, he catches sight of a digital camera that I have in my bag. He immediately forgets the aeroplanes. Well mannered as he is, he looks at me for permission before he takes out the camera. I suggest that we sit down on the couch so that I can show it to him. It seems natural to assume that he needs my help, but he opens the case, attaches the camera to its strap and hangs it around his neck. He knows exactly how it is done.

We got one almost like this at home. I know how it works. Dad has teached me. He takes loads of pictures.

Malte aims the camera at me and quickly snaps a picture. He shows that he knows how to take pictures, even though a major part of me is not included.

Your tummy taked up most of the space, he laughs.

He is having so much fun that he wants to take one more picture. He moves farther away since he has concluded that he stood too close before.

This one's mostly your tummy, too, but it's smaller now.

I smile and am happy that he is showing me the cheerful Malte, the one I have previously only heard about. He laughs when I say:

Now I think we have enough pictures of my tummy.

During our first three sessions, Malte expressed his traumatic experiences through different battles in the sand tray. But now I want us to begin to work on the book, so I suggest again:

Let's make a book about what happened. We don't need to draw. We can take photos of different dolls and things that we set up on the floor or in the sand.

Malte looks sceptical so I continue:

You can be the photographer so that we get pictures for the book. I'm going to write the words that should go on every page.

I want to show him that I am going to help him, and consequently I am more active than I have been at the previous sessions.

Malte gives me an affirmative nod but mumbles that he really does not feel like doing this. He shows at the same time that he both wants and does not want to get on board. He is unsure about how he can approach what happened in another way than talking or drawing, and he does not want to do either of those two. I assure him that we will help each other, he and I. My intention is to follow the manual for making a *Book about What Happened* when it comes to purpose and content, but the pictures will have to be photos instead of drawings. The manual suggests simple pencil drawings but Malte prefers more advanced techniques, so we will try using a digital camera and downloading the pictures on the computer. Granted I have never used this procedure in any therapy previously but why not, if it can awaken Malte's interest?

We use the major part of the session for Malte to think about how to take the pictures. We chitchat back and forth, and he gets a chance to snap a few pictures of toys and to look at them in the camera. He needs time to think things over before he feels ready to take on the work for his *Book about What Happened*. He creates that time by concentrating on the technical aspects of the project. He reverses our roles and now he is the one who tells me what I should do:

You can put the pictures into the computer later, 'cause then they'll get bigger. I know how to do that on our computer at home. I help my dad do stuff like that. You can do it on a computer like yours too, even though it's pretty old.

He points at my laptop, which is on the desk. He is quick to note its make and that it is old, which is more than I keep track of myself. When it is time to start working on the book I say:

This book is going to be called Book about What Happened, *and it's about Malte and what he's gone through.*

He wants to take pictures already, before we have even started, so I put the camera down beside us and tell him first that he may take a picture of each scene after it is built up.

I need to give him some straight talk:

I'll take out the camera when it's time to let you take the picture. There's to be a picture on every page of the book.

He goes along with everything that I say but he still looks doubtful and unsure about what is going on. I am painstakingly precise at this point because I want to help him dare to take on the work with the book. The book is a good method of daring to approach what Malte has experienced.

In the series of pictures, we will go through the entire course of events. I will only include those things that Malte's parents have told me he has said, and nothing that is only my or the parents' speculations. I will write the picture texts in capital letters. Every picture text will indicate that the continuation follows on the next page. When we get to the final step, the book will reflect the entire course of events. The aim is not to get Malte to remember more details, something I have explained carefully to both him and his parents.

Malte sits on the floor watching me and I try to interest him in what we can put together to illustrate this text. He does not do anything, so I fetch the boy doll that he has held in his hands earlier. We chat about whether this doll can represent Malte. He comments:

He's got the same hair anyway. Same colour, like.

Malte does not look uninterested, so I propose an opening scene for the story by placing the boy doll on a tricycle beside a little doll sandbox that Malte fills with a handful of sand.

Figure 1.1 I read the following text aloud while I write it on a piece of paper: Last summer when Malte was only four and a half years old.

In the first picture I want to underscore that we are going to make a book about something that happened a long time ago but is no longer happening now. To emphasize that the assault took place in the past, I choose things that can be associated with a toddler: a tricycle and a tiny sandbox. This is a concrete attempt to help Malte get a grip on the distance in time between the assault and the present. I direct the conversation to how things were for Malte when he was only four and a half years old. That was half a year ago, a long time when you are little. I let him tell me about whatever he wants. He shows me immediately that he would rather talk about his family than about what happened. It is important for me to listen without interruption at this point so that he will not feel that I am judging things he says as right or wrong. Malte says:

I don't know 'cause I had an ear ache. We've got a cat. Her name's Darling and she's got different colours on her. I know a stupid person who says she's ugly in a pretty way. Weird. I don't know what he's talking about.
What do you think of your cat?
She's nice. We've got six in our family – mum, dad, Johanna, Linda and Darling.

He shows me five fingers and after counting them with the index finger of his other hand, he notices that something is not right and he adds with a laugh:

And there's me, of course.

As children do, he naturally counts the cat as a member of his family. I ask if he thinks we should have a cat in the first picture. He lets me know immediately that he already identifies himself with the Malte doll when he says:

No, we can't 'cause Darling moved in with us after the summer. When it was autumn I was five and not four and a half.

Malte talks about his family and this talk makes him calmer. The thought of the book's content makes him anxious. We chat some more about his family, and he tells me that his sister Linda is ten years old and Johanna twelve and he adds:

I'm five now, not four and a half any more. That was a long time ago 'cause then I was in the Bluebell group at preschool and now I'm in the Cowslip group. You see what I mean? Next I'll be five and a half. Are you twenty years old?
No, pretty much more than that.
Oh really? What then? About eighty?

It is remarkable how hard it is for children to guess the approximate ages of adults. But Malte loses interest in my age when he catches sight of the camera. It surprises him that he has forgotten it while he has been so occupied with talking about his family. He snaps a picture happily and quickly. The picture is a bit crooked but that does not bother him when we look at it in the camera. Nor do I say anything because I do not want to risk having his attention more concentrated on the technical aspects than the psychological ones during our meetings. The session ends with my loading the picture into the computer according to Malte's instructions.

In the interval between this and the next session, I work hard with the camera and with the transfer of pictures to the computer in order to make this element of the therapy go smoothly. I cannot let Malte be disappointed now when he has found his own way of moving forward with the work. From now on, when each session begins, the pictures will already be accessible in the computer so that he can look at them. Paper copies of the pictures will be spread out on the table. However, Malte prefers to look at the pictures in the computer.

He bothered my weenie. It hurt.

Session 5

Malte squirms around a little. I write in the past tense here as well to show even more that what we are talking about concerns time that is no longer with us. Malte sits on the floor by the sand tray and looks at me. I go to the dollhouse and fiddle with the dolls. I take out some male dolls with different facial expressions, dolls that could represent Jack. I want to understand whether Malte harbours contradictory feelings toward Jack. Perhaps his choice of doll can tell me something about

Figure 1.2 I take out the camera and a piece of paper where I write at the same time as I read the text: A young man babysat for Malte and his sisters. His name was Jack.

that. I try to interest him in making a choice, but in the end the process of elimination rules. He rejects the one doll after the other until there is only one left. It is tall, wears jeans and has scruffy hair. I ask:

Do you think we should take him?
You decide.

Malte follows me with his glance but seems otherwise glued to the floor. Then I stand up straight and ask:

Where do you think we should place him in the room?
Somewhere, anywhere. You can decide.

I walk around the room with the doll that represents Jack, and I talk about different places:

Maybe in the dollhouse? Or on the shelf with the Indians and cowboys? Or here in front of the dollhouse? Or behind the cupboard, what do you say about that?

I want to be careful about bringing the Jack doll into the narrative. It therefore takes time before we decide together about what place he is going to get in the room and, consequently, later in the narrative. We come to an agreement that the Jack doll will stand in an out-of-the-way corner under the stairs leading up to the dollhouse. I associate this directly with the shame of standing in the corner. Malte cannot see the doll from the part of the room where he is sitting nor can the Jack doll see him. This is Malte's way of starting to build up a psychological distance to Jack and thus becoming able to approach the assault in his mind. I am struck by his inventiveness and am reminded of how the preschool teachers noted the same quality. I want to encourage him to take part on his own terms and agree:

Yes, I also think that's a good place for him.

Malte does not want to take the picture. Approaching Jack through the lens of the camera means getting too close.

You can take the picture, says Malte.

I do as he wishes and note to myself that I will load it into the computer after the session. I refer to Jack by name, and Malte says instantaneously:

He's nasty.

I agree with what he says:

Yes, what he did to you was terribly wrong and terribly nasty.

This is getting to be a little too much for Malte just now. He is agitated and scratches the eczema on his neck. I ask him if he wants to do something else and he does. He plays in the sand tray, but he cannot get any dynamic going and repeatedly interrupts himself. He starts over from new angles but nothing gets better. He tries to start battles where Indians fight against cowboys. Then he abandons them and goes on to make an explosion that represents a huge fire. A fire engine comes screeching in, but it cannot find the fire. Chaos rules. It is obvious that the mere thought of Jack distresses Malte. He gives up the game and complains:

It just gets messed up.

I suggest that he can come and sit down on a chair beside me, and I say:

Yes, things do turn into a "mess" sometimes when something bad has happened to you and you don't know how you should think about it.

When he has had a little rest I suggest that we can do another page in the book even though he might not really feel up to it.

Do you know what page it will be?
It'll be number three, right? says Malte and shows me three fingers.
Yes, exactly. You count exactly right.

I hand over the camera to him and suggest that he take a picture of the things he has left in the sand tray. He looks surprised and says:

But it's just a mess.
Yes, but in this book it's okay to put in a mess. Everything's okay to put in.

Malte says that I should take a picture. I take a picture of the "mess", which consists of an Indian who has fallen over, an explosion, an overturned fire engine and a little telephone. Since I am used to far greater "messes" in the sand tray, this one looks really minor. However, it shows that Malte is not used to dealing with chaotic and disorganized thoughts. The little telephone pleases me since it is a good sign of an expected continued dialogue between us. In the text for this picture of a mess I want to write something wrong that Jack has done. I will wait with what he has done to Malte in order not to rush things.

Figure 1.3 I read aloud while I write: Jack fooled around with his own weenie.

I am careful to use the same words and expressions that Malte used when he told his mum about what happened. I ask:

Was that how it was?
It's really crazy, isn't it? Malte answers and lies on the floor while he takes a big yawn.

This is how much of a strain the subject of Jack puts on him.

I agree with you. The whole thing's crazy.

Time is running out and so is Malte's stamina. We say bye to each other, and I promise that the pictures and texts will be ready in the computer by the next time we meet.

Discussion with Malte's parents

In today's discussion it is Jonathan who is toned down and Annika who is upset. She is thinking about the police interview and says that she has noted down everything she remembers of what was said. It is her custom to keep a diary. She has read through her notes prior to the meeting today. She needs to talk more about the interview and how it was not easy for Malte. Annika had spoken to him in advance about how important it was for him to tell things as carefully as he could. He had answered in monosyllables and had become unsure when the police officer asked him the same question over and over again. Annika thinks that Malte took this as criticism, as a sign that he was giving the wrong answer. Annika is just as upset as Jonathan was last time over the way a child has no chance against an adult. We talk about how this unfortunately is often the case when a child's word is pitted against an adult's. And there are never any witnesses, either. I say:

I see that Malte knows he has his parents' wholehearted support and that you believe in him. He knows these things because whenever he gets distressed he regains his comfort and security by talking about his mum and dad.

The parents are moved when they hear this, and I am moved by seeing them so moved over what I am telling them. We talk about Malte's feeling of insecurity, the way he no longer wants to visit the homes of children in his neighbourhood. He is listless, even though somewhat less than before. We talk about how it is necessary for them to be on the alert for when Malte wants to try going to his friends' homes again. They must help him to want to dare. I say so since his parents have become afraid to let him out of their sight.

Another theme is that Malte refuses to eat certain foods. On one occasion they got annoyed at him and insisted that he should eat all of his pasta, a dish that he has always liked. He had eaten it but said it was yucky, and after dinner he vomited. His parents felt guilty when they later understood that maybe Malte associated pasta with Jack since Jack's cooking skills were more or less limited to pasta. When Malte's parents speak at home now about what happened, they are careful to keep their voices down. The children stay calmer that way.

Both Annika and Jonathan describe how they bear a vague feeling of going around waiting for something. They do not know what it is, but the feeling is unpleasant. Earlier they waited for the police interview, which they thought would lead to the next step, a preliminary investigation, but then the whole thing was dismissed. They sound as though they are waiting to start to feel all right again. I want to give them hope until their own hope returns, and I therefore say with strong conviction:

Things are going to get better.

The parents are more composed today and less anxiety-ridden than the last time we met. Everyday routines have been partly reinstated now when Jonathan is back at work. They also see that things are going in the right direction for Malte. He has slept in his own bed three nights in a row, and during this last night, before the day of our meeting, he did not wet his bed.

He didn't say sorry

Session 6

When Malte comes to his sixth session he looks over at the computer. I put up the screen and show him the three pages of the book that are ready. After looking at the first picture he clicks quickly past the second one with Jack in it and looks at the third one with the "mess". He thinks it is strange to include a picture like this one. We then get started working on page 4. Here I want to put in something about what Jack did to Malte. I chat with him about the text that I intend to write. Malte is not capable of talking about this. He locks his lips. As I write the text I look at him questioningly to see if he has any objections.

Should we talk about it some more?

Malte answers unequivocally:

NO! Nothing.
It's really good that you can say NO. I'm writing that you don't want to talk about it. You're the one who decides. Great job!

Malte is obviously in a state of intense sensitivity, and of course I respect his wish not to talk about what happened any more. It is important for Malte to see that I respect his NO. Since Malte does not want to put any more time into this page of the book, I ask him:

Should we take a picture of only the sand?

The sand tray remains empty of toys today. This emptiness can symbolize "NO" and "nothing".

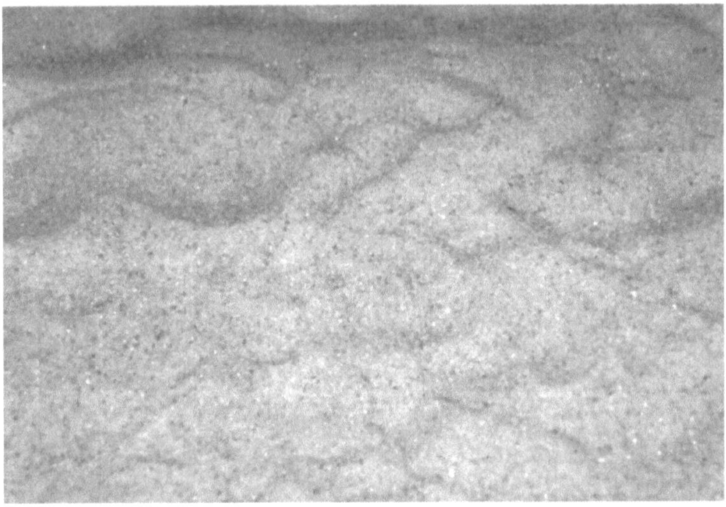

Figure 1.4 He does not protest when I read the text for him: Jack pulled hard on Malte's weenie. He jerked it around. Malte does not want to talk about it.

Malte nods in agreement. He brightens up a little bit and thinks it is just as strange to take a picture of only sand as of a "mess".

When we take pictures at home we always put stuff or people in them.
Oh, I see.
Yes, like my grandma.
You mean your mum's mum?
Yes. She doesn't want dad to take pictures of her close up.
Oh really, so she doesn't like that?
She thinks the picture gets smaller if you stand far away. All the pictures get big in the computer, you know. Weird, isn't it? Dad thinks it's really fun to take pictures of grandma. Then we all laugh.

After this we sit at the table and chat about everyday things, depending on where Malte leads the conversation. At the same time, we sort out the pieces that belong to a simple game. Malte is not especially interested in the game, but it is easier to talk if you have something to do with your hands. Suddenly Malte says:

Iris was the one who knowed him. He babysitted for her kids. She has two kids but only girls and they're too little. They's dad was ill and Iris had to go to work. My mum and dad also go to work. We were really s'posed to go to my other grandma, my dad's mum, but she was sick in her leg. That was stupid of her, too, you know.
Yes, you wanted to go to her house, I state and continue to listen to his narrative.

Dad says that Iris telled him that Jack was nice but he wasn't nice.

At this point I wonder:

Do you know what Iris liked about Jack?
He was good at hip-hop. My dad likes that, too. He could talk like Donald Duck. I also want to talk like that.

Here I sense that Malte misses the nice Jack, who had promised to teach him how to swim and how to sound like Donald Duck. I do not want to rush things so I say nothing about his perhaps missing the nice Jack. I save that for a later occasion.

We play the memory game for the remainder of the session. This game has the order and set rules that Malte needs now. You know what is right and what is wrong in that game. It does Malte good to spend time on something so uncomplicated. He has a good memory, beats me easily and is exuberant. He does not remind me to put today's picture in the computer when he leaves for the day. He trusts me to remember what to do.

Session 7

Malte wants to continue with the memory game when he comes in for the next session. He pours out all the pieces but we do not do much playing. Before I even hint at it, he understands that I am eager for us to continue with the book.

Okay, he says, and is ready to work.

I read aloud the four texts that I have written thus far while I show him the pictures and say that we are now on picture number five.

I know, Malte says, and shows me five fingers, three from the one hand and two from the other.

He is waiting for me to do something, so I take the Malte doll and put him in the sand. On this page of the book I want to bring out something about Malte's reactions to what happened.

Should we write about how Malte felt?

Suddenly he starts to talk about how Jack did not say he was sorry.

Here I want to assure Malte that there is absolutely no question about his own feelings of what is right or wrong.

Very good that you know that someone who has hurt someone else should say he is sorry. I see you know that very well. Good for you! But what Jack did to you is very, very wrong, even if he had said he was sorry.

Figure 1.5 So I write what Malte says: Jack did not say sorry. He did not.

Since I want to boost Malte's sense of being able to protect himself, I change the Malte doll's legs so that he looks like he is running and I say:

Now he can run away.

Malte is delighted and leans forward to change the boy doll's legs so that he can take even greater strides. He laughs gleefully:

Now he's running super fast; he's making a dash.

This part is fun and I agree:

It's really good that you can make a dash because then you can run fast to your mum or dad. You have strong legs, too, you know.

Malte agrees, pulls up the legs of his jeans and whirls his legs around so that I can see how strong they are. Then he rolls up his shirt sleeves to show me his biceps. I inspect them thoroughly from different angles. When he thinks that I have finished admiring his muscles, he puts his clothes in order again and I ask:

Do you think we should have any more things in the picture besides Malte?
No, but hurry up with the camera so that I can take pictures, he cries out spiritedly.
Right away, sir, I joke and mock-jog across the room to get the camera.

He thinks this is really cool. He takes the camera with a laugh, focuses it and snaps. In the first picture only the legs of his jeans are visible, and I say:

We see your strong and speedy legs but we don't see the Malte doll's legs.
Oh, don't we? Well, what's the big deal?

He thinks it is "cool" with a Malte doll that can dash away from the whole world. In the end, things are becoming a little too exhilarated, so I lend a helping hand by directing the camera toward the running doll. After the picture has been snapped, Malte says firmly:

Put me in the computer now.

Malte is bossing me around. This is his way of trying to reinstate his autonomy. No one is going to boss him around again. I pretend to trot over to the computer, which gives me some slight trouble. Before I have even done anything wrong, Malte notices that I am on my way to doing so.

You were about to press the wrong key, you know. Here's the right one.

We both have a laugh at the way he is one step ahead of me. When I do as he tells me, the picture of the dashing Malte doll pops up immediately in a large version on the screen. Malte becomes ecstatic with delight, takes some proud leaps in front of the computer, claps his hands and exclaims:

You did a great job there. Awesome!
Malte, you're the one who's awesome.

He is happy and thinks that both of us are clever, he at running fast and me at managing the pictures. I refer to his strong, speedy legs again and talk about them as an introduction to the sixth page of the book:

It's great that you ran down the stairs at home to tell your mum what Jack had done. I think you did so well there that I want to write it in the book.
Yep, that's what I did.

Here I want to underscore why Malte will never again be in danger of an assault from Jack. Malte himself plays an important part in this context. He dared to tell. He goes along with what I say and starts to think out the scene for the next photo. When I fiddle with the Malte doll, he takes it resolutely out of my hand. I wait in order to let him continue with his initiative and he does so. He tells me while he builds in the sand tray:

Mum was sitting there watching TV.

He places the mum doll in an armchair and finds a little TV that he puts in front of her. He is determined to put a rug under mum's armchair, but he has trouble and the furniture falls over. I help him so that everything stands firmly in the sand, but only in the way he wishes. It is important to let him decide himself how everything should be, now that he is ready for this step.

I make some suggestions for the text and after a little exchange of ideas we agree.

What's that stick? Malte asks and points to the exclamation mark.

We put in that mark when we think something very strongly. And I think very strongly that it was so good and brave that you told your mum what had happened. It was so good that I want to put one more mark there.

But Malte thinks I am overreacting because he says resolutely:

No, one's enough.

When we have come this far, Malte has experienced some kind of release. He is happier, moves about more freely in the room and tells me that they had a running race at preschool and he won, still another proof of his strong legs. After that he tells me that two of the children, who could not run fast, got angry. One child bit another child, who started crying and whose mum got angry. I understand that the preschool teachers have talked to the children about anger and about what you are allowed versus not allowed to do when you get angry. When Malte brings up the theme about being angry, I grab the opportunity.

Figure 1.6 I write and say aloud: Malte got scared. He told his mum. Good for you, Malte!

When a child is harmed, all mums and dads get unhappy and angry. They absolutely do not want this to happen. This is true with everyone at your house, too, you know. Your mum and dad have been dreadfully unhappy and angry. Your mum has been crying. Your dad has been both angry and sad because Jack hurt you. He's angry at Jack.

Malte is listening and I go on:

Your dad isn't angry at you or your sisters. Children can think their parents are angry at them if they think that what happened is their fault. Maybe your sisters also think they've done something wrong. They haven't been as happy as before. They don't even talk on their cell phones, your dad's told me.

Malte says that things have turned so strange, and he wants it to be the usual way again at home. I want to help him feel hope and I say:

It's going to be the usual way again. Okay, it's not possible for that to happen just now, but it will happen, I know that.

I sense that Malte, like many children in his situation, thinks that he has caused the tense atmosphere at home. He is perhaps still unsure about who is at fault despite all the assurances that the fault is never the child's. Suddenly he says in a shaky voice:

Grown-ups mustn't do stuff like that to little kids, right . . . ?
You are absolutely right, Malte. Grown-ups must never ever do stuff like that to little kids. What Jack did is something grown-ups are absolutely not allowed to do to little kids!

At this point Malte wants us to "play" a game that is entirely too advanced for him. We make our own rules as we go along and as we need them. The game is not important per se. Malte needs to have a little time to regain his composure before he goes home today. He does so by moving the pieces of the game several laps around the board. Malte's eyelids are heavy and he blinks. He is tired after this intense session. I say:

Sometimes therapy makes children tired.

Malte yawns widely, slides down from the chair and lands under the table. I lean my head down under the table and promise:

I'll fix the picture in the computer in time for our next meeting.

Malte is obviously tired as he walks out. He drags both of his feet after him but waves at me with both hands as he says:

Bye, bye, a big bag of byes.

Bye, bye, a big bag of byes to you, too, Malte. I'll be waiting for you next Tuesday as usual!

Discussion with Malte's parents

Annika and Jonathan talk about Malte's progress. They describe how he has become calmer at home as well as at preschool, where the teachers are seeing more of the old Malte again. His playmates wave and greet him happily when he arrives in the morning. He wets the bed less and less often at night time. His eczema is still there, but it is less aggressive and bothers him less. Malte has also had a play date with a neighbour child, something he did not dare to do one single time during the autumn. Jonathan only needed to promise to come and pick him up after one hour. Malte said that he had a good time. Annika says with a chuckle:

Now the girls fuss and fight with Malte again as usual. I guess this is a good sign even if it's no fun to hear it. They didn't say a single unkind word to him during the whole time he was so unhappy. They let him borrow their things whenever he wanted. That's all over now.

Jonathan adds:

And they chat on their cell phones as usual so now everything at home is back to the way it was before.

Jonathan has a lot to do at work and he is thankful for that. He no longer thinks so much about what happened.

At work they understood that something had happened. They asked me if my wife had left me or if our house had burned down. So I told them the truth.

I wonder:

How did they react?

Well, it's not something I can say in the presence of ladies, but every single chap gave me his support. They were mad as hell.

Both Annika and Jonathan feel a great deal calmer now that they see Malte feeling better. Annika has two new pupils in her class, and she is busy taking care of them. Lots of extra work is needed when new children arrive in the middle of the term, she comments. She, like Jonathan, is happy to be so busy. Work disperses their thoughts.

Their neighbour Iris, who knows Jack's family, has spoken to his parents and then related the conversation to Annika. Jack's parents are completely heartbroken and deeply shocked. Both of them have taken a sick leave. His mum does not dare to show her face in public. Jack has terminated his studies to be a teacher upon the admonishment of his dad. Annika concludes with a comment:

You know, his parents must feel worse than we do. I feel so terribly sorry for them.

We make the reflection that many people and families are made to suffer when something like this happens. Some type of help has been planned for Jack, according to Iris, but she does not know any details. Iris has naturally been worried that Jack might have done something to her little girls, who are three and four years old. When she has talked to them, they have just looked puzzled. However, in the final analysis, Iris does not believe that anything has happened to them because, if it had, she thinks she would have noticed. Jack has denied ever touching them in an improper way.

Annika wonders how Malte's twelfth and last session will be set up.

We would really like to come with Malte so that we can tie everything together.

I think the idea is good, but I will have to talk to Malte about it before we decide. It is important for him to express his wishes before we change our agreement. After all, we have decided that he and I will meet twelve times. We have written all the dates on a piece of paper, and after each session we have crossed out the day's date. That way it is easier to keep track of the number of times. I will get back to them with the decision about the twelfth session. I see two greatly relieved parents when they say thanks and goodbye today.

Grown-ups must never, ever do that, absolutely not!

Session 8

Malte knows that I have met and talked to his parents after he and I had our previous session. He does not have time to wonder about that now but goes immediately to the computer. He wants to see if I have kept my promise and downloaded his most recent picture. He opens my laptop and puts the screen in position with a deft hand. With the same natural skill, he clicks until he finds and opens the document entitled "Malte's book".

I read the texts aloud while we look at the pages of the book. I ask him if he remembers how many pages we have made. He looks offended, as though he thinks I doubt his memory. Malte has had a cold so two weeks have passed since we last met. In the next picture, which will be number seven, I want to enter into what is right and wrong when it comes to Jack's assault on Malte. He searches among the dolls and decides on two police dolls, one thin and one fat. He twists and turns the police doll with the fat stomach, the one who looks to be the more powerful of the two, and chooses him:

I want him.

Malte fixes up the police doll's uniform and standing position and considers how and where to place him. In the end he stands on some wooden blocks and holds up his arm in a stop signal. Malte looks in the cupboard for more things to put in the scene. He finds a train track boom that he lowers and places beside the policeman. This scene truly illustrates the lines of text that I want to write. A policeman makes a stop signal, and he is set up on a platform so that he is clearly visible. Added to him we have a lowered boom that blocks the way.

Figure 1.7 I read the text: No grown-up is allowed to hurt a boy's weenie. No! Not even if the grown-up was nice first. Not even if it was just for fun at first. The policeman says it is forbidden.

Malte examines the train track boom, raising and lowering it as he talks about how this policeman is different from the one he met at the interview. This one is more to Malte's liking:

He catches crooks and bandits and bad guys.
Yes, he does indeed. I can see that a mile away.

I read the text aloud one more time and add in a stern voice:

It's never a child's fault.

To underscore that it is absolutely forbidden, I raise my hand and make a stop signal just as the police doll is doing. Malte responds with the same gesture. He reacts to my stern tone of voice by listening attentively. He sits calmly and waits for me to say something more:

All grown-ups know it's forbidden. It's never a child's fault. Some children might think so but it's never that way.

Malte needs to hear more about how it is never the child's fault. He shows this by not ceasing to play with the police doll. He hums a song about a policeman, and when he is finished he says sternly:

Grown-ups mustn't do that. Absolutely not!
No, never, ever, I agree.
No, they mustn't. My mum says so, too.
What she says is absolutely correct. It's great you know that.

Malte wants to take pictures of the policeman from different angles. Most of all, he would like to get the policeman's fat stomach. But this page of the book is for accentuating what we have just talked about. I therefore suggest that we should take a picture of everything in the sand tray. He is eager to snap some extra pictures and I let him do so, even though I have said earlier that one picture is enough. In the introductory phase my purpose was preventive, to keep the technical considerations from gaining the upper hand. However, there is no risk of that now. Malte's curiosity about what will come on the next page of the book about his experience is firmly intact.

When we have finished looking at the policeman in the computer, we begin working on page 8. Here I want to write something about the consequences of what has happened and how things have turned out. I suspect that Malte wonders what has happened to Jack. He takes out the Malte doll and two children dolls that are playing with a doll hay wagon and a little skateboard. In the game he makes himself into the strongest child, who has the strength to pull the wagon that another child is sitting in. He is deeply absorbed in fixing and arranging the dolls.

Malte snaps a picture of the Malte doll and the other dolls, which represent his playmates at preschool. Malte now identifies himself with the Malte doll and tells me that the playmates in the picture are named Clara and Amir.

Malte has said at home that he is afraid that the nasty Jack is going to return. At the same time I seem to sense that he still misses the nice Jack. I therefore keep that theme going and talk about how we can feel like we both want and do not want to see someone again who has first been nice and then nasty. It is important for Malte to hear that people can have contradictory feelings. His facial expressions show that my hunch is correct. He listens and after a while I conclude our little talk by emphasizing that he and Jack are never going to see each other again. Malte has dreamt about new encounters with Jack and these dreams have turned

Figure 1.8 While he works, I suggest this text: Malte wants to play with his friends at preschool. Jack and Malte are never going to meet again.

into nightmares. For Malte an encounter with Jack is something neither to wish for nor to fear. His parents are going to make sure they never meet again.

It is possible that Malte thinks that he has tattled on Jack and that we should feel sorry for Jack. In order to remove any such erroneous burden from Malte's mind, I tell him what has happened to Jack:

Jack will go to a doctor who will help him stop doing things like he did to you. Jack isn't going to be a teacher.

Malte does not know how to react.

No one who does such things to children is allowed to be a teacher. He must work with something else. But first he must go to the doctor many times.

Malte listens in complete stillness. I want to tell him how I know this:

Your mum has told me about these things. Iris has told her. Your mum hasn't seen Jack, not Iris either. Iris is also angry and disappointed with Jack.

The thought of Jack distresses Malte, and he talks about his family for a while. The thought of his mum and dad has the usual calming effect on him. He says:

Mum and dad are at work today. Grandma came here with me. I don't know what they do at work. Talk on their cell phones maybe, anyhow mum does. She talks loads and loads. Dad works in a yellow house with big stairs. It's cool to be there. There's someone called Mrs Pearson at dad's job.

I wait while Malte retrieves one of his shoes that he has let slip off. He states matter-of-factly:

Mrs, I think that's a weird name.
So you think that's unusual?
Yes, Malte answers and indicates that he wants to talk a little more about Jack.
Jack played the guitar really good. We have a pool in our yard, and he blowed it up with just his mouth. Then we could take a swim.
Yes, you liked Jack in the beginning when he was nice.

Malte says neither yes nor no but he wants to hear more about how it is when a person who has been nice changes and turns nasty. To give him further support in the knowledge that we can have contradictory feelings, I talk some more about the confusion that such a turnabout usually creates. He needs to hear about this a number of times. Toward the end of the session I see that Malte is more relaxed.

Pippi Longstocking is an empowering role model

Session 9

On his way to my room, Malte hums the Pippi Longstocking song. As he leaps into the room on one leg, he sings with all his might:

Here comes Pippi Longstocking! Here I come! Yes, it's really me, Pippi Longstocking!

Standing on one leg, he tries to spin around and close the door. It does not work as he had intended, and he closes the door on one of his fingers. His only comment is "Oh, bother." Malte does not have time to concern himself with his little accident.

When we have looked at the eight completed pages on the computer, he goes over to the toys and takes out the Pippi Longstocking doll; her monkey, Mr Nilsson; and her horse, Little Old Man. When he puts his hands out to reach for the toys, I notice that the eczema around his wrists is barely visible now. It is only pale pink and does not seem to itch any more. He builds up different scenes from the Pippi Longstocking films that he often watches. He laughs to himself at first but is slightly clumsy and after some time gets annoyed at the toys for falling over.

I help him a little and hold the figures to keep them from falling. He knows exactly how he wants this scene to look. He wants Pippi to lie in her bed with her feet on the pillow where her head should be, as she always does. Little Old Man and Mr Nilsson are meant to be in the kitchen. He wants it all to be exactly like in the films. In the text for the picture that he is preparing, I want to underscore that Malte is a good boy through and through, with a right to his own integrity.

Figure 1.9 I weave the words into Malte's game and read the text aloud when I have finished writing it: Malte is a great kid. No one is allowed to be nasty to him. Malte likes Pippi Longstocking who is the strongest kid in the whole world.

Like many children who have been in frightful and vulnerable situations, Malte absolutely adores Pippi Longstocking. He has chosen a good role model indeed. No one dares to bother Pippi, since she is the strongest and richest girl in the whole world. She lives an exciting life despite the many crises that we must assume she has taken herself through, living without parents as she does.

Malte needs no help with the camera. He snaps a picture and looks at the image in the camera with the knowing glance of an expert and comments:

It's okay, it's totally okay.

Malte is delighted and claps his hands when we look at the computer and see Pippi Longstocking and the furniture from her house "Villa Villekulla". The chair is up on the table, Little Old Man is standing on the couch, Mr Nilsson lies in the doll's bed and Pippi herself is lying there asleep with all her clothes on and her feet on the pillow. Malte likes this sort of predictable disorder.

In the manual for making a *Book about What Happened*, it says that "when it is time for the ninth page, the psychologist should attempt to influence the child's self-image so that it includes joy, independence and strength, as well as the ability to protect himself and others." It is as though Malte has read the manual in advance because there is no better way of symbolizing all of these qualities than to identify with Pippi Longstocking. Before we conclude the session, I remind Malte that we have only three times left.

An old computer gave us good help

Sessions 10 and 11

At these sessions we talk a good deal about how we are soon going to conclude the therapy. Malte knows that it has to be concluded even though he would prefer to come some more times. I tell him that his mum and dad have said they would like to come with him for the last session. I wonder what Malte thinks of their request. After a little exchange of ideas between us, Malte says:

They can come a little bit. They can see the book.

We decide that they can come fifteen minutes before the end of the session. But we still have some time left before that.

The computer is set up with the slide show of the nine book pages Malte has created thus far. While I read through text line after text line, he browses through the pictures, also showing me several different ways of doing so. I admire his cleverness. Now, on the last page, I want to write something positive and hopeful about Malte's future. When he has gone over to the dollhouse and has started looking for various toys, I start the text by saying:

When Malte grows up, he is going to . . .

I stop there and hope Malte will illustrate his future by completing the half-finished sentence.

He fantasizes about one thing and another, makes a little mischief and laughs. I laugh, too. It is important to have a positive atmosphere now when he is planning his future. To give Malte confirmation for his ideas, I express interest in various details of his wishes. He changes his mind several times but he finally puts out the grandfather doll in the sand. Beside him he puts a bright red car and a dog. Money in the form of coins and bills is also included in the tableau. Malte is cheerful and excited and wants me to guess what he is thinking of becoming when he grows up. I think aloud about what it can be but, naturally, none of my suggestions is correct.

Your guesses are wrong, wrong, wrong. You have no clue. And this is the last picture. Number ten, Malte cries out and shows all ten fingers.

I want Malte to tell me his visions for the future in his own words since he no longer needs my suggestions. To put my curiosity to rest, he tells me and I write down what he wishes.

Malte takes a picture of everything included in his glorious vision and thinks it is even more exciting to see it enlarged in the computer. Now he is able to fantasize freely and fearlessly about better times to come. He would rather look ahead

Figure 1.10 I write down Malte's wishes for the future: When Malte grows up he first wants to be a grandfather. Then he wants to have a dog and a car and be a millionaire.

than back. I see this as an indication that Malte has regained hope as well as the sense of having control over his own life. I say:

It's good to have dreams of what you want to do when you grow up.

Malte wants to talk more about the future, even the future that is closer in time, and explains eagerly:

Granddad builded a tree house for me in his yard. He's going to let me sleep in it this summer. If it doesn't rain, of course. I don't want to get a cold.
No, of course not.

It is obvious that Malte adores his paternal granddad, who has always had a special place in his heart. During this painful time his granddad with his calm manner has also turned out to be a pillar of strength for the entire family.

"Give me five"

Session 12

For the last session Malte and I meet first. His mum and dad are going to come in after half an hour. Malte and I talk about how he felt about coming to see me in the beginning and he summarizes:

It wouldn't have been cool if I'd come to see anyone else.
No, of course not.

We talk through how it was after a time when we started working on the book. The whole book now exists in a paper copy, illustrated with excellent pictures in colour. It is lying on the shelf. I ask:

Do you want the book to stay here, or do you want to take it home?

Malte's answer leaves no room for doubt:

It should stay on the shelf.
Okay, then, I'll take care of it and keep it in a safe place.

We continue and talk about how things are going to be now when we will not meet any more. Ever since Malte really got on track for his therapy, he has enjoyed coming to it. At this last meeting I want to let him know that he has struggled valiantly. I compare how things are for him now with how they were when we met for the first time:

At that point you wanted to stop wetting the bed and you have reached that goal now. I know that you are sleeping in your own bed because your mum has told me so. I see from your hands that your eczema has almost disappeared.

Malte takes in my words with the greatest solemnity. I save what I think is the most important for last:

And you can play again. You didn't feel like playing when we started meeting. You had forgotten how to play. Now you think it's fun again. That's the greatest.

Malte understands what I mean right away in the manner that children usually do when they hear this. All children want to be able to play. It is purely and simply vital for them.

As arranged beforehand, Malte's parents knock on the door after thirty minutes. They are interested in what has made it possible for their son to become his old self again. Malte fetches the book with all ten pages bound together in perfect order. He shows it to his mum and dad, but he holds it and turns the pages himself. He has learned all the lines of text by heart so he "reads" them aloud while he turns the pages. When he comes to a couple of the more painful pages, he turns to the next page a little faster. In contrast, he gives his parents a little extra time to look at the pictures toward the end of the book, the ones where he has been more actively engaged in deciding the content.

Perhaps this is Malte's way of showing that he has come through the worst of the crisis and that neither he nor his parents need to think about it so much any more. Malte has been concentrated in his efforts and has worked himself out of this chaotic experience. His wish to let the book remain on my shelf after his therapy is over is perhaps a sign that the matter is closed and can now be "put away on the shelf". He does not want to take it home with him.

I admire Malte for his bravery and freedom of spirit when he shows the book to his parents. Jonathan says that Malte and he have not talked so much because he has understood Malte as not wanting to talk. He is moved and says that he takes it as a token of confidence from his son that he has been shown the book. We talk about how Malte understands that his dad is not angry at him. And, besides, Jonathan is not angry any more at all. In answer to his parents' question about what we have done, Malte and I, I reply:

The book summarizes what Malte has worked with during his therapy. It has been necessary for your son to work through his experiences in some way other than by talking or drawing.

Annika and Jonathan nod in agreement when I make an observation about something that they already know:

Malte likes technical equipment like computers and digital cameras so we have used them instead of crayons and pencils.

Malte's dad sounds delighted when he says:

Typical Malte. He's a clever kid when it comes to computers. He's taught himself, mostly by checking out what I do.

His mother concurs cheerfully:

He's going to be a technology nerd, just like his dad.

I remind them that I am going to contact them for a follow-up after six months to hear how everyone is feeling. All three of them look relaxed when the session is over. Malte clings to his dad to delay the parting moment just a little. While we are saying goodbye to each other, Malte bounces over to his mum's handbag, takes out an envelope and gives it to me. It contains a card where Annika and Jonathan have expressed their gratitude for all the help. On the front of the card Malte has drawn a picture of himself driving his red dream car. His head sticks up above the steering wheel. While I thank them for the beautiful card, I give Malte an amused look and say:

Thanks so much, Malte. And you're the one who says you can't draw.
Yes, but that was when I was five years old. Now I'm five and a half.
Oh, of course. Now why didn't I think of that?

Malte reaches out toward me with the palm of his hand open and says:

Give me five!

I give him my "five" and then he and his parents say in unison as they go:

Thanks and goodbye!
Goodbye!

Six months later

I have sent Malte's parents a form in advance with different questions about how Malte feels now. I read their answers before contacting them by telephone. It appears that the family members have found their way back to their everyday life again, which I am pleased to know. When I call, one of Malte's sisters grabs the phone and shouts for her mum. In the background I hear a thud and a screech. I wait while Annika takes the phone to another room. She says laughingly:

As you can hear, there's a lot going on, so everything's back to normal again. Malte's eczema has disappeared and that's the best thing of all. It was driving me crazy.

Malte's other symptoms have faded away and have not returned. He sleeps in his own bed and stays dry all night. Annika adds:

He's become better at standing up for himself, especially when his sisters try to boss him around. But we've been wondering, how do you know when a child has finished working through a thing like this?

I reply with a counter-question:

Does Jack often come up in the conversation in the family?

Annika says:

Malte mentions his name now and then. He does so even though he doesn't seem to be interested in talking about him beyond that.

The parents are uncertain about how they should deal with this and we talk about it. I share my experiences, which are that children can believe it is wrong of them to stop talking about something that has upset their parents so greatly. The parents in turn can believe that it is good for the child to get a chance to talk some more. I conclude by saying:

I don't believe that Malte has any particularly great need to talk about this any more. He's gone through it here in his therapy and with you. After all, he also seems to feel all right. What's more, I'm sure that you'll notice if he ever wants to ask you or Jonathan anything in particular about what happened.

Annika concludes by thanking me for phoning her and saying that they do not think we need to meet again. I end by asking her to give Malte and Jonathan my best regards. I would have liked to meet the family again for a more extensive conversation but therein lies the psychologist's dilemma. The ultimate goal of our work is to render ourselves unnecessary. Sic!

Sexually violated children

The mere suspicion that a child has been subjected to a sexual assault evokes extremely painful and overwhelming feelings in the adults who are close to the child. The thought of such an assault is every parent's nightmare. They warn their children, telling them never to let themselves be persuaded to do anything by a person whom they do not know. But when someone in the family's inner circle violates a child, everyone experiences total shock. Both the child and the parents are filled in different ways with overpowering feelings and reactions that are difficult to handle.

The adults experience feelings of such intensity, as they have never known before. To find out that someone has deliberately harmed your child arouses profoundly primitive feelings including shock, chaos, panic, violent aggressiveness, vengeance, powerlessness and despair. The child's trauma becomes the parents' trauma. Consequently, the parents can also need professional help to work through their reactions and to support their child in the best way.

A child who has been sexually violated has been made to endure something overwhelming, both physically and psychically. In order to have any chance whatsoever to withstand this attack on his body and his autonomy, the child often undergoes a loss of sensory and memory impressions. A feeling of unreality emerges that confuses the child. Afterwards it does not appear obvious to the child that what has happened to him is a part of reality. For certain children, as for Malte, some time elapses before reality catches up with them and they can show signs that something has happened. Only then does everything come to light for the first time. In addition to being shocked by what has happened, the parents are troubled that it has taken so long for the child to say something, seeing this as a lack of confidence in the parents. But a child cannot tell about such an overwhelming experience before he has begun to understand that it has actually taken place.

In many cases children might say something on one occasion and then not be able to bring themselves to say any more. They might have answered the questions at the police interview to the best of their ability, but after that, they have no more to say. It is difficult for a child to talk about a sexual assault, which is such an alien experience. Perhaps the child has protected himself by closing off sensory impressions and feelings, or perhaps he is confused and has a hard time remembering what has happened. In addition, a preschool child does not have the vocabulary to cover what has happened.

Many times children do not want to cause more turbulence in their family and their surroundings by saying more, since they are often unsure about their own role in the course of events. It is also difficult for adults, who are full of their own strong feelings, to be sensitive listeners for the child and to help him express what is on his mind. This is true not only for parents but also for professionals who are not psychologists. When children come to a psychologist for therapy, they believe that they are expected to give details about what happened. They have been told that they are going to get a chance *to talk* to someone who can help them.

However, it has a calming effect on them when they realize that they do not need to talk if they do not want to. There are many other ways to communicate with children about experiences of this kind. When a traumatized child starts in therapy, he is first given a chance to express his experiences through, for example, drawing, painting, playing with toys, playing games and building in the sand tray or the like. It is usually not any problem for children who are given a psychological space to express themselves symbolically and in that way convey what they have experienced. A child psychologist is also adept at picking up what is "between the lines" in the child's symbolic language, which makes it easier to get a full picture of what has happened.

The next step, where the difficulties come prominently to the surface, is the working through of the feelings and reactions that are behind the psychic symptoms. To eliminate these, the child needs help to dare to approach the trauma, from both an emotional and a realistic side. The child must understand that he has gone through something real in order to be able to put the experience into words. It is thus a matter of turning the experience into something "speakable" after it has only been "playable". The psychological tool *Book about What Happened*, which I used in Malte's therapy, can play a valuable role in this process. In a firm but gentle way it helps the psychologist to lead the child through the trauma. The child thus dares to approach the dreadful thing that has happened. It is gradually possible to talk about the experience, and it no longer traumatizes the child or the parents. At this point, the psychic symptoms are reduced. The child and the parents can talk about the assault as something dreadful that happened, but they can handle their feelings.

Psychologist Bengt Söderström, who has constructed the tool *Book about What Happened*, has also written a manual to go with it. There he suggests that the book can consist of ten pages with an exemplarily simple illustration and a line or two of text on every page. The texts clarify the pictures. Every picture elucidates in chronological order a certain phase in the course of events. In words and pictures the little book covers the entire trauma in the way that the child has chosen to express it. The narrative starts before anything bad happened and ends with thoughts toward the future. The trauma is thus "packaged" into life as a negative but confined experience. By these means the child understands that this is a closed chapter and that life can go on without any more similar experiences. The purpose of the *Book about What Happened* is not to make the child remember more details but rather to help him find his way back to the person he was before the trauma occurred.

2 How long will she be dead?

Ronia, seven years old, comes to crisis therapy several years after her mother's death

Everyone else has a mother

One afternoon, three weeks after the autumn school term has started, an e-mail arrives from a dad named Peter. He writes that he is contacting me because he needs advice about his daughter. Since I do not like to have e-mail with sensitive information about children, I write back and tell him to call me instead. We talk on the phone, and he tells me with sadness in his voice about the difficult situation that has unexpectedly arisen in his family. He wonders how he can best help his daughter Ronia, who is seven years old and has recently started her first year of school. She is the younger of his two daughters. Her sister, Anna, is three years older. With her there are no problems, but Ronia refuses to go to school now because Peter has told the new teacher about Ronia's mother's death. Ronia had forbidden him to say anything about this at school. Ronia's mother died five years ago when Ronia was two years old.

I make an appointment for a first visit with Ronia's dad and ask him to bring Ronia with him. First he answers yes, but then after a short while he becomes doubtful that he can get his daughter to come along. She is angry most of the time now, says no to everything and screams that she hates him. I suggest that he explain to Ronia about the appointment. The two of them are going to a place where dads and children receive help so they can be happy again. I also ask him to tell her what my name is and that there are things in my room that children like, such as a sand tray in which she can build. Most children find this set-up enticing. It is important that Ronia is present for the first appointment. She must be given a chance to know what I already know and to listen to what her dad has to say. She has already shown that she reacts very strongly when he "goes behind her back" and talks about her mum who is dead.

To me it sounds like her teacher's finding out about her mother's death has merely been a triggering factor for Ronia's reactions and hardly the whole reason for them. In order to instil confidence in Ronia so that she can get the most out of meeting me, we need to put all the cards on the table. Peter says, though, that if it becomes too much of a strain to get Ronia to come along, he will just come by himself. He feels entirely too exhausted and at his wit's end from all of Ronia's heart-rending outbursts. I conclude the conversation by asking him to greet Ronia from me and to tell her that I am looking forward to seeing her and her dad next Wednesday at two o'clock. I sense that I am going to meet a sad little girl, not an aggressive and angry one. It may be that feelings of sadness and loss toward her mother have caught up with her now.

In my narrative about Ronia I describe our two first meetings thoroughly. I also explain at length why I suggest crisis therapy for her several years after her mother's death. My talks with Peter are given in summary form. From Ronia's therapy sessions I choose to describe a selection of all the sequences that illustrate her hard work to regain her joy of life.

Session 1. Conversation with father and daughter

When Peter arrives with Ronia the first time, he is holding her firmly by the hand. He does not let go of her until we greet each other and shake hands inside my room. Peter is in his forties, has combed-back brown hair and brown eyes and a gaze that shows he is both secure in himself and unhappy. Ronia is a cute, long-legged seven-year-old with blue eyes and medium-blonde, medium-long hair. She is wearing a sweater that once was red but now is faded. The child gives a pale impression. The father and daughter are strikingly different appearance-wise.

Ronia waits until her father has sat down in one corner of the couch before she sits down in the other corner. Judging from Ronia's expression and from her dad's firm grip of her hand, I expect that she has not been delighted about coming here. Ronia does not know how she is going to react to the fact that she is now sitting in a room with her dad and me, a total stranger. She has an angry expression around her mouth but her eyes are sad when she looks in my direction from under her fringe.

Well, here we are after a few rounds of arguing, says Peter.

I turn to Ronia and say:

It's so good that you came too. I sat here and waited for both of you. Please feel welcome.

I start by saying again that my name is Elisabeth. I say what I know about why they have come to see me:

I meet lots of children and dads who have had sad things happen to them. Your dad has called me and told me that your mother died when you were little. He has also told me that he wants to get help so that the two of you can be happy again. I can help both of you with that.

Ronia gives me a blank look. Peter intends to speak but I signal to him to wait a moment. First I want to tell Ronia everything that he has told me. If Ronia is going to develop trust in me, she needs to be sure that her dad and I are not talking behind her back. I continue a bit longer:

Your dad has also told me that you don't want to go to school. He told your teacher that your mother is dead. You didn't want him to do that. And now you don't want to go to school any more. Your dad is very sorry about that. I don't think he really understood how important it was to you for him not to talk about your mother.

I told him not to say anything. You're so stupid, says Ronia.

She is turned toward her dad and she looks almost as if she means what she is saying.

Yes, I do feel stupid. I don't understand what's going on because everything has gone well for Ronia during all her years at day care and preschool.

Before we continue I want to tell you, Ronia, that what you and your dad tell me stays in this room. I'm not going to tell your teacher or anyone else.

I ask Ronia, who is still peering at me from under her fringe:

Do you think we should let your dad tell us why he wanted the two of you to come here?

She gives a barely discernible yes-nod in response, so I let her dad take the word. Peter does not know where to begin. He clears his throat and starts hesitatingly:

It's difficult to lose your mum when you're as little as Ronia was. She was only two years old. Her big sister, Anna, was five and she has memories of her mum, so it hasn't been as difficult for her.

Ronia sits still and listens as her dad continues the narrative. She does not seem to have any objections so far to the way her dad is describing what happened. Peter talks about Ronia's first year and what it was like.

My wife, Hanna, got ovarian cancer when Ronia was two months old and Anna was three years old. Hanna's mum stopped working, and she and Hanna's dad, who was already retired, took care of the children as much as they could manage. Hanna was in the hospital for long periods of time.

After a glance over at Ronia, who is starting to become agitated and is kicking her feet, Peter hesitates and I interject:

If you want to look around the room, Ronia, please do so. You can hear what we're talking about anyway.

Peter continues:

I stayed at the hospital a lot, and it was a considerable distance away. I wouldn't have been able to handle everything without the help of my in-laws. It was hard for them. It was a tough time for all of us, but no one believed it would turn out the way it did, not we ourselves and not the doctors. We had bought a house before Ronia was born. I also had to work since we obviously needed the money. I wasn't doing well anywhere, not at work, not at home and not at the hospital.

When Peter has said what he wants to say, I request of him:

Tell me about Ronia when she was little.

Peter answers:

I can't because I was living in a vacuum. I don't remember anything from that time, nothing at all. I have only fragmented memories of the children. I don't remember world events or what was current then. Nothing! But grandma has written down in a book when the children learned different things and everything else imaginable. Grandpa has made a nice photo album from that time that we often look at.

He concludes by noting sadly:

Ronia got a difficult start in life.

I really want to get Ronia involved in the talk so I say:

That's so nice that you have your grandma and grandpa because then you know what it was like when you were little. Do you remember anything that Grandma has written about you?
Yes, she wrote that I could crawl fast.

Her dad adds:

But you learned how to walk when you were a year and a half. That's what Grandma has written. I've heard that children who are together with unhappy people aren't so fast in their development.
Well, maybe so, but Ronia, what do you think about what your dad is saying?

Ronia is now sitting in my swivel chair and is turning round and round. She slows down, looks at her dad and says quietly:

It's okay.

It is clear that she has heard all this before, and she no doubt often thinks about how everyone else has a mum but she does not.

Everyone will find out

Peter continues and says that the situation for the family has now changed radically. He has met a woman with whom he and his girls have recently moved together. They have moved from a smaller town to Stockholm just in time for the autumn school start. They have found a spacious flat that he is in the process of renovating. Peter wanted to move fast so that the children would not miss school, even though the flat is not quite liveable yet. His fiancée, Carolina, has three sons, Anton, Rasmus and Ludvig, from two earlier relationships. They are all school age and have already been attending the school that Anna and Ronia have just started. Two of the boys, Peter says, are sometimes with their dad over the weekend. The dad of Carolina's oldest son, Anton, is dead.

I am also eager to hear a little about Ronia's sister Anna, even though it is Ronia whom Peter worries about. Peter comments that Anna has more of a temper and shows when she is sad or angry. She is more stubborn and says what she thinks. Here Ronia mumbles:

Yes, you can bet your life she does!

Anna has told Peter's fiancée several times that she is not their mother so she has no right to tell Anna what to do and not her sister either. And that's that! When Ronia hears this she giggles. She clearly thinks that it is gutsy of her sister to say so. Carolina thinks that it is easier to understand and deal with Anna. She thinks, as Peter does, that it is easier for children who have some memories of the deceased. When Ronia's dad has finished talking about Anna, he turns to Ronia and says:

With you I don't always know, but I have thought things were all right. Now I don't know any more.

Ronia has draped herself over my swivel chair on her stomach and moves the chair back and forth in rhythm to the way I am talking. Turned toward the chair and Ronia, who starts to spin round and round on it, I say:

Your dad wants things to be good for you. Now I want to hear what happened when your dad told your teacher about your mum, even though you didn't want him to do so.

It takes some time for Ronia to finish spinning. She drags it out even more before she comes and sits in a chair next to us and says:

Dad can tell you.

Peter sighs before he starts talking about how things have turned out for them at this point:

Ronia's school start has not gone well. Everything's new, the school, the teacher and her classmates. At school she goes into sudden temper tantrums, rips up her drawings, throws herself on the floor, screams and cries. Ronia doesn't know why this happens. One time she kicked the teacher on the leg.

When Peter says this, Ronia adds quietly:

It wasn't on purpose.

I interject:

No, Ronia, I'm sure it wasn't.

Ronia was there when the teacher told Peter what had happened. She also said that Ronia was unhappy and did not seem to like school. She asked if there was anything in particular that his daughter needed help with. Peter had said that he did not know. He told Ronia's teacher that her mother had been dead for several years, that they had recently moved to the area and that Ronia did not know any other children yet. He also said that Ronia had been happy during her day care and preschool years. The teacher had promised Ronia that she would get to sit next to another girl in the class who also did not know any other children. That girl also really wanted a friend.

When they returned home after the talk with the teacher, Ronia completely lost control. She panicked, threw a tantrum, cried and screamed. She sobbed and cried all night. Everyone was terrified and did not understand what was going on.

We tried to talk to you. We tried to ask you what was the matter but you didn't hear anything because you were crying so loud, he says, turned toward Ronia and continues: *I nearly had a breakdown myself. I was completely destroyed when I finally understood why you were so upset. You didn't want your teacher to know that your mother is dead.*

Ronia says:

It's ruined now.

At first Ronia cannot verbalize what has been ruined, but she looks as if she means that absolutely everything is destroyed. I ask her:

If you think about it a little bit, maybe you can figure out exactly what is ruined now that your teacher knows.

The others will find out. She will tell them. They always do.

Oh, I understand. And you don't want that.

Peter's eyes are welling up with tears as he listens to his daughter. He says:

We both cry at night time. I have not been able to sleep since all this happened. I feel like a traitor. She didn't want her teacher to know. I knew that but didn't take it seriously. Maybe I shouldn't have said anything but that wouldn't have been right either. No matter what I had done it would have been wrong.

I agree with him and think to myself that what is wrong is *the reason* behind what Peter told the teacher, not *the act* of telling her. The fact that Ronia's mother died is what is super wrong.

The life lie

Peter blows his nose and continues:

I don't know what to do. Of course Ronia has to go to school. She says she never wants to go there again. We've stayed home the last few days. I can be with her at school and just sit there quietly, but she doesn't want that either.

I look at them both and want them to tell me something about mum. Peter is the one to start:

Hanna was kind, adored her children and collected old glassware. She was a nurse and died when she was thirty-two years old. Ronia has her mother's colours, blue eyes and medium-blonde hair. Hanna's parents are from Finland, but Hanna was born in Sweden.

Ronia listens with a look of recognition on her face. She comments from time to time, and it sounds as if she remembers what her dad is talking about. But gradually I get the impression that father and daughter have an unspoken agreement that of course Ronia remembers her mother. Can it be so? Or is it mostly for Dad's sake that Ronia "remembers"? He shows clearly that he wants it to be that way. But Ronia's mum was in the hospital for long periods of time before she died and Ronia was only two years old then. I do not comment on this either but instead intend to wait until a later occasion when it is more fitting.

It is calm and quiet in the room. No one says anything for a while. All three of us sit there absorbed in our thoughts. Father and daughter look emotionally stricken and sad. After a while Peter wants to share a beautiful memory he has of Hanna and Ronia. I see from Ronia's body language that she knows what he is going to say. She has heard it before. Even before he has time to start talking she huddles herself up in the chair and snakes her arms around her head. With her fingers she covers both her ears and her eyes. She blinks and fights to keep the tears back. When Peter sees what she is doing, tears start streaming down his cheeks.

He suffers for his daughter and for his own powerlessness, but he does not connect her actions with what he is about to say. He pats her on the back but Ronia does not reciprocate his attempt to approach her.

Peter shares his memory with me:

Ronia remembers the last time she saw her mother. It was at the hospital. Hanna didn't have any hair. Ronia went up to the bed and hugged her. It was such a sweet moment.

Ronia has put herself into a fetal position and is completely still. A long, long silence follows and Peter waits for a reaction from his daughter. After a while, in order to conclude what he was talking about, he says:

It was like that, wasn't it, Ronia?

Ronia jumps abruptly out of the chair, bolts across the floor and lands right in front of her dad. She is distraught, angry and sad. Everything at the same time. She cries heart-wrenchingly, and in-between sobs she screeches her protests right into her dad's face.

No, I did not, not at all.

She sobs and her nose is running.

Oh yes, you did. That's the way it was, says Peter.

No, it wasn't like that at all. I didn't do it. It was Anna, screams Ronia between her crying attacks.

Peter is both bewildered and horrified by his daughter's sudden explosion. Ronia never had a tantrum like this before she started school. Peter has a hard time giving in; plus he is sure that his memory is accurate. He tries a last time in a pleading voice:

But we talk about it often, about how you hugged mum.

It wasn't me who did it. You stupid head. I just can't believe how stupid you are. You don't understand anything.

Ronia is now screaming straight into his ear. Her whole body is tense and she is as upset as she is sad. Her dad does not back down but becomes more and more teary-eyed. Ronia looks so small and heartbroken as she stands there crying. Her tears gush out and her nose is running. I put some tissues on the table so they can wipe their eyes and noses. Peter hands a tissue to Ronia, which she does not accept.

Ronia has gone along with everything her dad has said up to now. But not this. She did not hug her mother the last time they saw each other, and now she is simply unable to keep this to herself any longer. She has heard this story many times but enough is enough. I am guessing that with the best intentions, the family have tried to create a life story about Ronia and her mother. Within it is the story about the last hug. But that story is not true! It is a life lie. Ronia has known all along that it was her sister who gave that hug to their mother. Ronia did not want to.

Peter stands up and lifts Ronia into his lap but she squirms her way out. They remain seated in their respective couch corners until Ronia has calmed down. Her dad feels rejected, but after a moment he puts his arm around her and does not let himself be stopped by her now less passionate protests, which subside after a while. He pulls her toward him so she lands in his lap. He speaks comfortingly and wipes away both his own and Ronia's tears. I feel strongly for them both. They are in the same boat and totally dependent on each other. Neither of them can understand the situation that has arisen or handle the feelings that it has awakened.

After a few minutes I think I detect a certain relief in Ronia's face even if she looks very, very tired. Clearly she has never spoken up about this before. Until now she has kept quiet about her knowledge about the lie. Now she has seized the opportunity to speak the truth. In order to manage that, she has had to have a child psychologist in the room plus muster all her courage. She has made her dad understand that the hug is a lie and nothing else. It is not an authentic memory. When the atmosphere in the room is calm again, time is up. I conclude by suggesting that they come back one more time so we can talk more about how I can help them.

Before we say goodbye I want to show Ronia what I have in a cupboard that she has not looked at yet. There are hand puppets, finger puppets, miniature dolls, drawing paper, paints, games and some other odds and ends. She picks through the contents absentmindedly and then looks down at the sand tray and the things that children can use to build there.

I wanted to show you these things so you know what is here next time we meet. But now we have to wrap it up for today.

In the meantime, Peter has walked out into the hall so we join him and I say to them both:

Okay, so I'll see you next week. You're welcome to come at two o'clock on Wednesday. By then school is over for the day. Go back to school now, Ronia, because I want to hear how things turn out. I want to know if you get a seat next to the girl who wants a friend, and I'm curious about what her name is.

Ronia yawns widely and leans exhaustedly on her dad. I suggest that for the next meeting the three of us meet first, then Ronia and I will meet alone and finally Peter will come back. I want to talk to Ronia alone.

Peter looks worried as they walk down the steps hand in hand. Ronia is so tired that she trips over her own feet. Ronia and Peter have shared how difficult their lives have been since the death of Ronia's mother. They have given me a lot to think about. The visit has lasted longer than I had planned since I wanted to make Ronia curious about different things in the therapy room. The air is heavy, and I hurry to air out the room before my next little visitor arrives. I also take a moment to jot down things from Ronia's visit that I want to think about again later. I make a note of Peter's conversation with the teacher and his guilty feelings toward his daughter. I see the helplessness they share after the life's lie exploded like a bomb, and I see their plea for help.

Not easy being a little sister

Session 2

When Peter arrives with his daughter for the second session they rush up the steps alongside each other. Ronia points out where they need to turn after they reach the landing. Peter sits down in the same couch corner as last time. Ronia sits down in a chair and looks at me. They are both out of breath so they have probably rushed to get here in time. Ronia's socks have almost slid off her feet. When they have caught their breath I ask:

Is there anything in particular you've thought about since we last met, Ronia?

She answers quickly as she inhales:

Nope.
How about you, Peter? I ask.
Well, yes, I've thought a lot about how things were for Ronia when she was born. She came into a life of chaos right away. It's crazy when I think about it. I can't believe that we've managed as well as we have.
It must have been really tough for all of you, both children and adults, I say.
Yes, and of course it's harder for a baby than for a three-year-old when their mum becomes ill. Everyone thought it was easier to help Anna. At least you could talk to her.

Peter sits quietly absorbed in his own thoughts, as does Ronia, while she looks at my shoes, which have a shiny buckle. Peter seems to think that it is very important for the children to have a memory of their mother. He says that he has managed thanks to all the practical help he has received from relatives and friends. He says that Anna received help in a children's group under the direction of the church and that he has spoken to a lay assistant at the church, who has been a good support for him. Ronia always enjoyed day care and preschool. She has been liked by the other children as far as Peter knows.

But I've always had a guilty conscience about Ronia. I have not been able to help her enough since my energy has been needed just to hold myself together. Yes, that's how it was during Hanna's illness and the year after her death.

Ronia has heard this before. Peter picks up the thread about his older daughter again:

Anna got to join a group with children in her same situation. It was really good for her. Where we lived there were a few other children who had also lost their mother or father, so the parish put together this group. They met several times. Anna was six years old then. It was one year after Hanna's death, and after meeting with the group Anna had a successful school start.

At this point, Ronia, who is barefoot now, stands up and interrupts her dad. She is turned toward me and says animatedly:

She got to go there ten times. That's what they got. Anna said it was fun and she met Andrew there. When it was the last time, all the parents and brothers and sisters got to come. I was invited, too.

I listen to everything she has to say about the help that her sister received and then ask:

Oh, a kind of party? What did you and dad do there?
All kinds of stuff. Talked, played and got lemonade and then we got really good sweet rolls.

Peter agrees:

Yes, I must say that the church did a good deed for us there.

I think he is right when it comes to Anna but not to Ronia, who wants to tell me more:

They got to draw and write letters, too. They got to send them to whoever they wanted. It didn't matter if they didn't know where they lived. They made their own stamps, too. Really pretty ones. And then there were funny hats. We have pictures of them.

It sounds like Ronia has the impression that all the sad children except for her got to experience the togetherness of that group. She was only three years old when Anna went to the group, but it is clear that Anna's experiences there have stayed with the family. Ronia might remember some things herself, but most things can probably be traced to later remarks or to the pictures she has seen from the last time the group met, where Dad, Anna and Ronia are all dressed up in funny hats. Ronia has obviously felt alone and left out. This is often the case for the youngest sibling. Everyone wants to protect that child, and many times we are unsure of how to help a child who has barely learned to talk.

In order to conclude the remarks about her older sister and instead draw the attention toward Ronia, I ask:

What do you think about the fact that Anna went to that group?

She passionately repeats what she has previously stated:

She got to go ten times. She did!

There is an undercurrent of accusation in her voice that Peter detects right away. He takes what she says to heart and guiltily tries to explain:

There was no group for such little children as you were then, Ronia. You were too little, and when you got older there were no groups at all.

The conversation now takes entirely another turn. Ronia feels accused of being too little. She becomes angry. More angry than sad this time. She stands up in front of her dad with her hands on her hips, puts her head on the same level as his, stares him squarely in the eye and hisses into his face:

I am not little! You don't understand anything! I am not little!
I haven't said that you're little now.
But I know you think I am!
I was talking about when you were little.

Ronia counters right away with tears in her eyes:

Everyone treats me like a little baby!
When you were two years old you were little. Not now. Please stop, dad says pleadingly.

Peter is being extra patient with Ronia because he is eager for her to feel comfortable during the visits and to want to come back. She does what children usually do – takes advantage of the situation and continues to nag about not being little. She can sense that her dad does not want to raise his voice when they are with me. In order to help Ronia pull herself together I say:

You were little a long time ago. Now you're several years older. I think you want to be even bigger and happier just like your sister, who got to be in a group where you were left out.

Ronia mumbles something about unfairness while she looks at my shoes, which she seems to like. Maybe Ronia associates the word "little" with the death of her mother. Every time she is treated like a little child she is reminded in different ways of her loss.

The conversation becomes entirely too much of a strain for Ronia. She cannot take all this talk any more. She does not know how to deal with all the thoughts and feelings that have been awakened such a long time after her mother's death. She wants to do something else, build in the sand tray or open the cupboard that she looked inside last time. Peter looks deflated and says he will go outside and wait. He thinks it would be good for Ronia to be alone with me for a bit. This was indeed what we decided at the last session. I look inquisitively at Ronia and she responds:

Yes, wait on that chair where we were sitting.

She means the waiting room.

Yes, let's do so and then you'll return when we have ten minutes left of the session. I will want to talk to you both then about how I can help you more.

Okay, I hope it'll work, says Peter and continues: *I need help. I cannot bear to live in the past any more. I want to go on with my life with Carolina and my girls and her boys. I want that more than anything else. I wish I could make it happen. But it feels pretty hopeless when the first thing to happen is all this.*

When her dad has left the room, Ronia opens the cupboard with all the toys. She gives me a cautious smile, rubs her face and carefully examines the puppets, the paints, the wild animals, the dolls and the games. She takes her time, twisting and turning the toys. When she has looked at everything she goes to the sand tray and looks at the things that are there: cars, tigers, trees, little dolls, cabins, furniture and Indians. She sits quietly and peacefully, slowly examines all the toys and strokes the sand with her hand.

She puts out a few train cars in the sand tray but changes her mind and removes them. Maybe it did not turn out the way she expected or she did not finish thinking before starting. She is probably used to having to hurry and then nothing turns out the way she expects it to. She digs for a while in the sand with a shovel and fetches a bucket that she fills with sand, only to pour all of it out soon thereafter. When she does this, she seems like a much younger child.

Ronia thinks the sand tray is fun, but she does not really know what she wants to build in it. She takes her time and needs to think about it once and once again before she decides. She sits calmly and potters around with the objects. When I look at her back I get the sense that she really enjoys getting the time she needs. She shows the work pace that suits her. She does not have her own watch nor does she look at the clock on the wall. The passing of time seems to be something she would rather not think about. The room is wrapped in stillness, and I simply say matter-of-factly:

Here you don't have to rush.

How nice, says Ronia and looks contented.

After she has thought about it for a while, she starts building in the sand tray and lines up the brown fence pieces in a straight line in the sand. They get to function as train tracks, and on the tracks she places an engine, after which she connects a long line of train cars. She takes her time to arrange it all so that the tracks, the engine and the train cars are all in a perfectly straight line. Not a single little crack is noticeable between the fence pieces and none of the train cars is in the least crooked. She is more interested in having everything be perfect than in driving the train (see Figure 2.1).

I notice that Ronia needs to go to the restroom so I point to the relevant door and say:

If you want to go to the restroom, it's right there.

Ronia prefers doing one thing at a time and cannot concentrate on going to the restroom now but instead pinches her legs together. I have to accept her priorities, but I suffer with her. After a while I ask:

What have you built?
A train that's out taking a ride.
I see. Where's it going? I wonder in interest.
I don't know. Nowhere.
Where do you think?
Somewhere maybe. I don't know, is Ronia's answer after thinking about it for a minute or two.

Her indefinite answer is right. She knows little about where the train is going, in the same way as she knows little about which path to take in her own life to move things forward.

Shortly before her dad rejoins us I ask Ronia if she wants to come see me more times. First she looks a little surprised at the offer, but then she says she would like that. At that point her dad knocks; Ronia looks at the door and I say in a raised voice: "Come in!" I then ask Ronia to come and sit with Peter and me, and I explain:

We have important things to talk about so your dad and I also have to hear from you about what you're thinking. The important thing we're going to talk about is how I can help you and your dad.

I continue:

I see that both of you need help. There is help available that will make you both feel better. I suggest that you, Ronia, continue to come and see me and you, Peter, also come a few more times to talk to me. Your dad needs to talk about how he can make things good for his younger daughter.

Ronia perks up and Peter nods and says:

Yes, it's really Ronia's turn now.
And yours! You have a big job ahead of you, building up your new family plus supporting Ronia through this crisis, I say.

I reassure Ronia that she gets to come and see me TEN times, as many times as Anna went to her group meetings. That means eight more times. Ronia has clearly shown that the number of times is important to her. It also makes things fair between the sisters. In addition, I judge that ten times are sufficient to help Ronia work through her delayed grief reactions.

Turning to Ronia, I speak slowly and with pauses:

There are many children who come and see me who've had someone in their family who died several years ago. Those children haven't been sad the whole time. They've been happy, too. But they become sad again when new things happen in their lives. Children usually like it best when things stay the same, and they can need help to want to get used to those things that are new.

I am thinking about Ronia's life situation, which has changed so much in such a short time. She says quietly but firmly:

It's not mum who's the problem. It's school.
Yes, I understand. It's good that I know how you're thinking.

Ronia looks at me from under her fringe and seems satisfied with the fact that I accept her reason for continuing to come and see me. Children and parents do not always see the same reasons for a child's need to seek psychological help. The reasons are usually connected, but they are just expressed differently. I continue:

Children who come here get help to become happier. And then they usually want to get to know new classmates and want to get used to new things.

Before we shake hands and say goodbye, I ask Peter to call me when Ronia, he and Carolina have talked through whether they can manage, practically as well as psychologically, to get Ronia to her therapy every week. For this, time must be set aside in the new family's already intensive schedule. Peter gets appointments to talk with me a few Fridays. Wednesdays at two o'clock are Ronia's time, eight more times. That makes it a total of ten times. Peter is determined:

I'm going to make sure that Ronia is here every single Wednesday at two o'clock. I really appreciate the chance to come on those Fridays because I want to get our life in order.

Peter does not quite dare to trust that Ronia is going to want to come back. The expression on his face signals this to me. Myself, I have no doubts at all, so I nod encouragingly toward them both. Ronia is going to want to come back. She shows that she has made up her mind once and for all. When they walk down the steps she is gesturing wildly and speaks eagerly to convince her dad of something. She is also keen on letting him know that she has decided what she wants to do next time. She sounds convincing and maybe she is afraid that her dad is going to hesitate about coming back. Both of them sense that the upcoming appointments will not be easygoing. They are coming to take on a big job, to be carried out by playing or talking about the most difficult subject of all. The loss of a mother.

Why crisis therapy for Ronia several years after her mother's death?

As a treatment form for Ronia, I suggest crisis therapy, or, as it is called in our professional literature, time-limited short-term therapy. I judge this form of therapy to be the most appropriate based on what I have seen and heard, directly and indirectly, during our two meetings. I also consider such factors as I can sense on my own, based on my experiences from many meetings with children in crisis and chaos. I summarize here why Ronia needs psychotherapeutic help in order to work through her residual grief reactions after having lost her mother.

Ronia is a downhearted and grave child who seldom smiles. She makes a sorrowful impression. She does not notice how her clothes are placed on her body. Her jeans and socks are soiled and should have been changed several days ago. In the past she has not shown particularly strong feelings about her mother's death but instead has been described as a rather contented child. She was tense and curt initially in her contact with me, but she has become less and less reserved and shows that she wants to make an effort, both at talking and at playing. Ronia needs to be able to take her time when she is going to think about something. She shows how she prefers her existence to be through the way she carefully builds a train track in an absolutely straight line. She cannot cope with major sidetracks or surprises, not for the train and not in her own life. She has managed to maintain her inner psychic balance as long as life has gone on as usual, each day just like the one before it.

Ronia's existence has been put through great changes over a short period of time. She has suddenly been put into an entirely new life situation that she has not chosen herself. In actual truth, she has not said anything at all about what she thinks about everything. She has moved from her own room, from her preschool class, from the children in her neighbourhood, yes from everything. She has previously had a room of her own but now she must share with Anna. She has started at a new school with a "stupid" teacher and classmates whose names she does not know. Last but not least, she has also become part of an entirely new family constellation with her dad's new partner and her three sons. Everything is new and uncertain, thus bringing the loss of her own mother to the fore.

Moreover, both her dad and Anna have changed. They are no longer the way they were before. Her dad is happier since deciding that they should live together with Carolina. Anna thinks everything is exciting. But Ronia's big sister, Anna, is more like Peter, and the two of them seem more robust than Ronia. She cannot take on their ways of relating to things, and thus she cannot have them as her models of how to act and be. She cannot accept the fact that the two of them have become happier. Now she has given her dad a reason not to be happy any longer. He looks unhappy for the most part. Ronia feels guilty about this, which adds to her unhappiness. Now both she and her dad have feelings of guilt toward each other.

Ronia goes to school because her dad tells her that she is not allowed to stay away, but she goes there in a joyless frame of mind. Peter has asked the teacher not to say anything about Ronia's mother. The teacher understood and promised, but Ronia still has not got over the way her dad let her down. She has fits of despair in the evenings, screams and cries about something she has failed at or destroyed during the school day. According to her dad, she has not learned her classmates' names even after four weeks. As I see it, in the years since her mother's death, Ronia has not been able to create sufficiently tenable psychological tools to manage situations that awaken feelings of loss and abandonment.

By tenable psychological tools I mean that children need to find their own strategies, ways of relating and behaving and new ways of thinking that can help them in stressful situations. The strong reactions that are evoked in Ronia when someone in her new life has found out that she has no mother show that she has not succeeded in creating such tools. The situation thus has become entirely too hard for her to handle. She cannot relate to it, and therefore the feeling of being betrayed will not go away.

Perhaps Ronia feels that her dad is not the only one who has let her down but that her mum has done so as well by leaving her. I think that during the meeting with her teacher, Ronia suddenly understood that she could not flee from her own past. It follows her like a shadow no matter where the family might move. Perhaps she had hoped that she could start anew and, as a part of that, no one would know that she was motherless. In order to cope with everything that is new, I believe that Ronia wonders how long death lasts and how long her mother is actually going to be dead. The insight that she will never come back is entirely too cruel for Ronia when she is so vulnerable.

The memories of her mother that people have so painstakingly tried to give Ronia have never been her own, and she has felt that. Many have spoken to the sisters about their mother Hanna, about how clever, kind, beautiful and well liked she was. Ronia has taken on the role of remembering her mother, not least for her dad's and her relatives' sake. Everyone has seemed pleased and less worried when the girls have shown that they remember their mother. Ronia was quite young when this started, but children are aware from an early age of how their behaviour affects others. She is close to her dad and does not want him to be unhappy, but not too happy either.

Peter and Ronia have a close relationship, so close that they cannot always distinguish which feelings and memories belong to the one or the other of them. What stand between them are Peter's un-worked-through feelings of guilt about not being adequate as a dad. He needs help to get on the right side of these feelings so that they can cease to burden him. He has really done everything in his power under extremely difficult circumstances, but he himself does not feel this way.

However, what troubles me the most is that Ronia sends out "feel-sorry-for-me" signals. When people see her, their first impulse is to think of her as a poor little motherless child and to pity her. She wants these pitying glances to go away, but she does not understand her own role in making people see her as little and helpless. This intensifies her anxiety.

Ronia does not want to be treated as a little child any longer. Just hearing the word "little" upsets her since it leads her thoughts back to what happened when she actually was little. Ronia wants to be seen as the schoolgirl a child of her age is expected to be. She wants to be able to cope with school and her new family life. She wants to be able to concentrate so that she can learn the names of her new classmates and make a best friend. She does not want to feel alone. She does not want to make her dad unhappy. She talks intensely about the help her sister received, and she is curious about me, my things and what I have to offer. Here she shows, in the way a child does, that she wants to get help.

Many people have done their best to help Ronia. She has been "subjected to" plenty of well-meaning but gloomy attention. Perhaps people have been a little too quick to console her and come with explanations without taking things at her pace. Ronia must take herself through her delayed reactions of grief, but she is entirely too torn in different directions and anxiety-filled to manage on her own at this time. What I have described here forms the basis for my conviction that Ronia needs professional help. She needs this help to find her own modes of expression for her feelings and to create her own memory images that are meaningful specifically for her. Crisis therapy will give Ronia good help, even though several years have passed since the catastrophe took place. Her grief reactions manifest themselves first now in connection with other severe stresses. It is urgent for Ronia to receive psychotherapeutic treatment so that her grave and downhearted manner does not need to become a lasting personality trait.

Okay, but no busybody talk

Session 3

I meet Ronia and her dad in the hall outside my room when she comes for her third visit. At this point Ronia is tuned in to the idea that she is going to get to see me ten times, and she knows that there are eight times left. Peter starts to say something about one of Ronia's appointment times. She pushes him on the back and hisses:

No, dad, you can't ask Elisabeth to take one of my sessions away. I say no! You already told her it was okay! You said that! You said that!

He explains:

One of the times it's going to be hard to get here. I have an important meeting at work.

I do not think it is a good idea to start out by cancelling one of Ronia's sessions, so I say:

We've promised Ronia that she gets to come here ten times, so it's good if we can keep it that way.

I am thinking of how Ronia has shown me so definitely both in her games with the train and through her reactions that she cannot take any more changes if she is going to gain a sense of security. The building up of a secure platform is exactly what I want to start with in therapy now. For Ronia it is extra important to be given clear frames in both time and space so that she will dare to use the sessions to the fullest. Peter catches himself at the same moment as he mentions his meeting. This is exactly the kind of thing that gives him a guilty conscience – not having enough time and energy for Ronia. His job often comes first. From the look on Peter's face I see that what I said has hit home, and he responds immediately:

Yes, of course.
I hope you can change the meeting when you know about it so far in advance.
I'll fix it.

Ronia lights up for a brief moment when she hears that her meeting is more important than her dad's. I want to make it perfectly clear that there are not going to be any changes with her times, and I say:

You and I are going to meet ten times. There are eight more times, counting today.

To confirm this, I stretch out my hands and extend all of my fingers. Ronia also wiggles all of her fingers around behind her back and counts them silently.

Peter goes to the waiting room, and before Ronia and I go into my room to start the session, she looks at me, points her index finger at my nose and says to me in a harsh tone:

Just don't give me any busybody talk. No nonsense, okay?

It is no problem for me to agree with her.

No, of course not. I don't like that kind of talk either!
Good.
I don't like busybody talk, either, Ronia. We have important things to do as we know, and we're not here to talk nonsense.

To show in another way that I respect her request, I make a move to shake hands with her. However, she prefers a more modern way of sealing a promise. She reaches out to me with an open palm and says:

Give me five!

I respond by pressing my palm against hers and nodding in affirmation.

I wonder what makes Ronia want to forbid busybody talk and why she uses the particular word "busybody". Is she referring to the many people, no doubt mostly of the female gender, who have tried to console her but who have not really given her the support she has needed? She is absolutely earnest when she gives me such a harsh warning before I have even had time to start any busybody talk. To underscore that we have important work to do and are not going to talk nonsense, I turn on the red "Do not disturb" sign outside the door and turn off the telephone. Ronia observes me closely during this procedure. In the sessions immediately following this one, she automatically checks out the door sign and the telephone. Thereafter she trusts me to indicate that we are occupied and do not want to be disturbed.

Ronia now knows how many times we are going to meet, and this makes her less tense. She sits on a little child-sized chair and looks around the room. She becomes even more composed when I let her know that she does not need to hurry. I encourage her to look around the room, and I tell her that she may choose what she wants to do. I wait for her to take the initiative. In therapeutic work we always let the child's choice of activities or toys lead the way. Ronia considers what she wants to do. She puts an index finger in her mouth and looks at me to see if I have the patience to wait. I give her a friendly look and wait calmly until she figures out what she wants to do:

I wanna set up the trains today as well.

She sets up the engine and the train cars on the fence tracks in the same way as last time. At first, she places the tracks in a perfectly straight line. They must not be allowed to take any curves, and just as before, the fence pieces must be without openings in-between. She takes apart a train track that she has made before she sets up a new and identical one. She does so several times, and I say:

Here it's not like at school or at home. You don't have to clean up. It's quite okay for you to leave things in the sand tray if you want to. Then I can look at them later because I want to remember what you've built.

She does not hear anything. She is totally absorbed in her game of making identical train tracks. She continues to take away the one before she builds the other, the new one. Ronia prefers to do one thing at a time. Otherwise things get too messy for her. All of the trains move in the same direction, and I comment on what I see:

Ronia, I think you like it best when the trains go forward on a straight line and don't take any winding turns.

Ronia looks like she finds my observation to be correct. Perhaps she grasps that I am referring not only to the trains but to her entire existence that is no longer on track. She does not say anything. Instead she takes out a train track boom that

Figure 2.1 The train chugs straight ahead on the train track without winding in or out. The track must not have any curves since the train must move along in an absolutely straight line. Ronia shows that she likes it best when life goes along at a calm pace. But recently her life has taken many wide and winding turns. She has not had an easy time.

she lowers in front of the train so that it has to stop. In this way she shows that her words, just like the game, have come to a temporary standstill. The train stands still behind the lowered boom, and Ronia sits just as still as the train. She looks as though she is thinking of something related to my comment. I leave her in peace with her thoughts. It is not easy for Ronia to find words to express why the train cannot go any farther. Something else is stopping it because she could simply raise the boom otherwise, but she does not.

It impresses me to see how diligently Ronia stages her own situation of not being able to get any farther. In therapy she must pause in order to understand what within herself is in her way. She needs this understanding to be able to go on with her life. After a time I talk to her for a while about how it can be hard for both trains and people when their energy disappears. She listens intensely to what I am saying, and I hope that she is not categorizing it as busybody talk. But I believe that Ronia has already noticed that our meetings have a different content from other conversations she has had in the past. She does not understand how this will help her, but I see from her trusting look that she is beginning to trust what I say and do.

Suddenly we hear stamping on the stairs. Ronia comes to attention and looks toward the door. I explain:

There are other children who come here, and now they're running up the stairs.

I make use of the opportunity to remind her that there are several children who come here because perhaps they know someone who has died and that they are unhappy because of that.

When are they all going to come? Ronia asks.

At first I do not understand what she means, but after a couple of seconds or so it strikes me that despite all my explanations she has perhaps expected to meet a group of children here in the same way that Anna met with a group. I explain that she is the only one who comes to see me on Wednesdays at two o'clock. No one else. The other children are here to see other people. She looks satisfied and says:

Oh, so that's the way it is. Okay.

Ronia is keyed up about starting her therapy. She needs to relieve herself badly and rushes to the restroom. Her discomfort is so great that she does not have time to be afraid of the dark when she does not find the light switch immediately. She returns from the restroom with her clothes in disarray. She does not notice it and I do not mention anything. She shows here that she is not so careful about how she looks. It is possible that she feels just as much in disarray inside herself. The last train track for today is set up a little less carefully. Ronia places the train cars a bit crookedly and the fence pieces are not as perfectly laid out. The boom is still lowered over the track so that the train cannot move. She is tired and lies down on the couch until the session is over. She is yawning as though the tiredness inside her is endless, when I tell her that our time is up for today.

Session 4

When Ronia arrives for her fourth session, she runs up all the stairs and waves and smiles as soon as she catches sight of me. She sets up the train tracks and plays with the trains but places less importance on putting the tracks in perfect order. She varies her train game and puts a church near the train. Beside the church she places some tiny dolls that are completely neutral, with neither facial features nor gender. When she chooses to place these particular dolls in the sand next to the church, Ronia does the same thing as many other children with her experiences do. Such a scenario is a way of daring to approach the thought that someone is actually there at the cemetery. Using anonymous dolls makes this thought less frightening since this "someone" is still not specified.

With Ronia I am careful to be especially patient and discreet. I cannot let her perceive herself as being treated in a childish way since she is so sensitive about that issue. I show that I am interested in whatever she is doing or talking about. For long periods of time I leave her in peace with her games and thoughts. Now and then I talk to her back. It can be easier to listen under such circumstances, and after all, she does not need to look at me in order to hear what I am saying. It is not that she is uninterested in my words but rather that she is absorbed in what she

Figure 2.2 The train's forward movement gets freer. It takes quick turns and moves both fast and slowly. Some little wooden dolls lie beside a church. There is a train boom that can be opened and closed.

Ronia's play shows that it is less important to be so careful. She is trying to adapt to her new circumstances. She is testing how it feels to be freer in her way of looking at the world around her. Her growing flexibility is a sign of more good things to come. The little neutral dolls that are lying beside the church show that she dares to think about death, even if it is not yet connected to a definite person.

is playing. She appreciates being given time and finding me interested in what she is doing without asking too many questions. There has to be a calm and accepting atmosphere around Ronia. During a major part of the session today, I take an active part in what she is doing but without speaking. We will have time to speak to each other during the sessions to come.

Hard work and joyful play

Session 5

The first thing Ronia notices when she comes to her fifth session is what I am wearing on my feet:

Where're your shoes?
I have another pair today. These are also mine.

Why? The other ones are nicer. Did you throw them away?
No, I have them at home.

Whenever Ronia does not see a particular thing that she is expecting to see right away, her first thought seems to be that it is gone forever. This is possibly true for people as well. Since Ronia has declared that she does not like changes, I say:

Next time I'll wear the shoes I usually wear.

My comment puts her at ease and she starts to fiddle around curiously with the toys. I take a quick look at her shoes. They have lost their shape and flop around without her noticing it.

She has become less and less concerned about being so meticulous with the trains. She now takes some dolls on a train trip, choosing an older couple, whom she calls Grandpa and Grandma. Her play shows more variation. She uses both dangerous-looking bears and huge explosions. After a certain hesitation, she lets an Indian woman with a baby in her arms ride in a train coach. Ronia bends her back and forth.

Figure 2.3 Tracks are no longer needed. The train takes quick and wide turns and still finds its way. Dangers are lurking in the form of wild animals and an explosion, but traffic signs help to keep things in check. An Indian mum with a baby rides in the caboose. She falls off the train, gets back up, falls off again, and it goes on like that.

Ronia is impressive when in her play she stages her hopes that her mum is trying to come back. After all, no one has said that her mum is going to be away forever. She also shows that she is facing new possibilities and that her surroundings are less frightening.

The trains are finally allowed greater freedom of movement outside the tracks and she says:

The train doesn't need the tracks. It's too much work to build them up the whole time. The train can go without them.

I say:

Does the train know which way it should go?

Ronia responds by making the train do sudden sharp turns in the sand.

Maybe the train doesn't know what's there behind the curves, I say.
But there are roads signs, she says, and points to the signs that she has put out.
Yes, I see. That's good because then the train driver can look at them. That way he knows how he should drive to get to the right place.

She runs the train so fast that the Indian woman falls off. While Ronia fixes the Indian mum and the baby, she talks to herself and makes associations. She says for the second time, straight out into the room:

Mum's not the problem. School's the problem.
Yes, I answer, speaking to her back. *I know that's what you think, and I'd like to hear more about your thoughts.*

I show her that I am prepared to listen to her thoughts about why we are meeting. Even though I try not to sound pushy, it is obvious even to me that I sound that way. Ronia does not answer. She has had enough of people with expectation in their voices, people who want to get her to talk. She thinks for a long time but something in her closes up. She wants to answer but does not come up with anything to say. However, I see her desire to try to answer as a step forward.

Everything in the room is at a standstill until Ronia goes over to the desk, puts the Indian woman on my computer and says:

She's s'posed to sit here.
Yes, I'll take care of the Indian mum and her child. I'll check on them every day. They'll be sitting there when you come, if that's what you want.

Ronia impresses me when she, in her play with the trains and the Indian mum with her baby, stages how she is struggling to take command of her own life history, the fluctuations of her existence and the various choices of direction she now faces. All of this takes psychic energy. She looks content but is markedly tired when the session is over. On her way down the stairs she trips on her shoelaces and falls down but quickly gets back on her feet again. She looks around to check if anyone has seen her fall. No one has seen, luckily for her, because she does not want to be regarded as a clumsy little child. The content of Ronia's therapy alternates between happy play and hard work, as she works through the difficult feelings that have remained inside her, several years after her mother's death. The healing process must take this course since things otherwise would go too quickly and painfully for Ronia. She is, when all is said and done, only seven years old.

Discussion with Ronia's dad

During the course of Ronia's and my meetings up to this point, Peter and I meet for two talks. He wants to hear how things are going for his daughter. I tell him how Ronia appreciates getting a chance to work at her own pace and not being hurried. I also say that she looks pleased when the telephone is turned off and no one is allowed to disturb us by knocking on the door. We talk about how children of today can never count on adults to refrain from answering a call on their cell phone, even if they are in the middle of an important talk with a child. Peter says that he no doubt should show Ronia more undivided attention and give her more time, if their new life is going to work out. I tell him he is right.

Ronia still calls Carolina "dad's girlfriend" and does not like to be alone with her. We say that Ronia will no doubt get closer to her after she has worked through her feelings in relation to her deceased mother. Carolina has put her foot down and said that they must either concentrate all their efforts on building up the new relationships or on making over the new flat. They must choose. She says that it is unrealistic to think they can do both, and Peter agrees with her. As a result of their discussion, Peter has contacted a building company that is going to renovate the flat instead of their doing everything themselves.

Peter wants to talk about what he can do for Ronia now. He says that he is tormented by guilt feelings toward her, even though everyone says that all the problems stem from his tough situation. I suggest:

You can start with small things. Let the time on Wednesdays after therapy be Ronia's and your time. There's a nice café down the street where you can go, just the two of you, without the cell phone.

Good idea, I hadn't thought of that. Well, is there anything else you can think of?

Yes, it would have a good effect on Ronia to come to therapy in good time, maybe by a margin of fifteen minutes.

But we usually do come on time, Peter says in defence.

Yes, of course, but Ronia needs a little more time to sit down in the waiting room, tune herself into therapy and use the restroom.

Peter nods and I continue:

Ronia also seems to need a little more help with the way she dresses. She cannot always see the difference between clean and dirty on her own.

Oh, my goodness, thanks for telling me! What the hell's the matter with me? I seem to be blind to the obvious. One of the boys said the other day that Ronia needed to wash. Then I also noticed that a shower would do her good.

We return several times to the new situation that Ronia faces. The break-up from her old home and surroundings plus other changes have brought the loss of her mother to the fore. Peter is so eager to get on with life and to do so together with his two children. He can no longer stand living in the past. His mood is much happier than it has been in several years. It was a shock for him that Ronia would react as she has done. Peter realizes that when Ronia's teacher found out about her mother's death, this was only a triggering factor for Ronia's despair. However, just within the last few days, she seems to have become somewhat less reserved. Peter repeats several times that he really wants to commit himself to a future together with Carolina, his daughters and her sons. He wishes with all his heart that things will go well for the new family. He wants to get settled in the flat and puts great effort into dividing everything as fairly as possible among all five children.

Peter comments that Anna and he have come through their grief but Ronia has not. His daughters are not in sync with each other. He is grateful that it is now Ronia's turn to get help but also says sadly that he has not understood earlier that she has not felt good. We conclude that Ronia no doubt has felt as good as she has been capable of but then a point has arrived at which she could not go on that way any longer. I tell Peter that in her games Ronia makes an effort at wanting to cope with changes. Carolina also thinks it is good that Ronia is getting help. She had wanted help for her oldest son when his dad died, but it had not been possible to arrange.

Mum got ill because I was in her stomach

Session 6

Today Ronia and her dad arrive well ahead of the appointment time. Ronia has time to use the restroom, and Peter reads aloud from comic books in the waiting room. In this way Ronia gets a calmer start going into her session. As time goes on she loses interest in digging and building in the sand tray. She no longer has a need to do so. The bucket and the shovel are left to rest in their place, as are the trains, tracks and booms. I continue to give Ronia my undivided interest, and she has become attuned to the rhythm of the sessions. She likes her therapy and has become more and more interested in our talks and in how she can express herself through play.

I am wearing the shoes I had from the beginning, but now she is looking me in the eyes instead of looking at my shoes. She does not care about them any longer, and she cares just as little about the "do not disturb" sign. But if I were to have overlooked the one thing or the other she no doubt would have noticed it immediately. However, at this session I have overlooked something more serious! I suddenly notice that the Indian mum with her baby is not standing on the computer. I always take her away after Ronia's sessions because another child comes in after Ronia, and she also wants her important objects set up at various places in the room. Today I have neglected to put the Indian back in place. I notice that Ronia has seen the empty space without mentioning anything, and I say:

The Indian mum's not where she's supposed to be.
No, she's not, I know, Ronia answers.

I see that the doll is lying in the toy cupboard, but I choose not to fetch her right away. Instead I want to use the opportunity to talk about another mum who has disappeared. I say:

She was always supposed to be there.
She's gone, Ronia says matter-of-factly.
How do you mean?
She's disappeared. But maybe we can find her, she says to me in a comforting tone.
But I'm the one who has promised you that here things will be as they usually are. I know that it's important for you.

The conversation reaches a standstill for the moment. Ronia does not know what she is going to say and neither do I. I do not come up with the best way to avail myself of the symbolism surrounding the missing mum because I am so disturbed by my guilty conscience. How could I forget that mums should always be where they are supposed to be?

Instead, Ronia plays in the dollhouse and rearranges the furniture and the dolls that live there. She puts all her energy into fixing up a room with a bathtub in the middle of the floor. Armchairs and couches are set up all around it. She chooses a mum doll that gets to lie in the bathtub. She puts a shower hose and nozzle on the doll's stomach. A dad doll sits at the head end of the bathtub.

I wait until she has finished arranging the room before I ask her what the dolls are doing.

That's some kinda machine there, she says, and points at the shower hose and nozzle.
What's the machine for? I ask.

I suspect that the mum is doing something other than taking a bath.

That's so you get air, Ronia answers.
Oh, I see, and we need air so we can be alive.
It's broken, I think, Ronia continues.
How does it work if it's broken? I wonder.

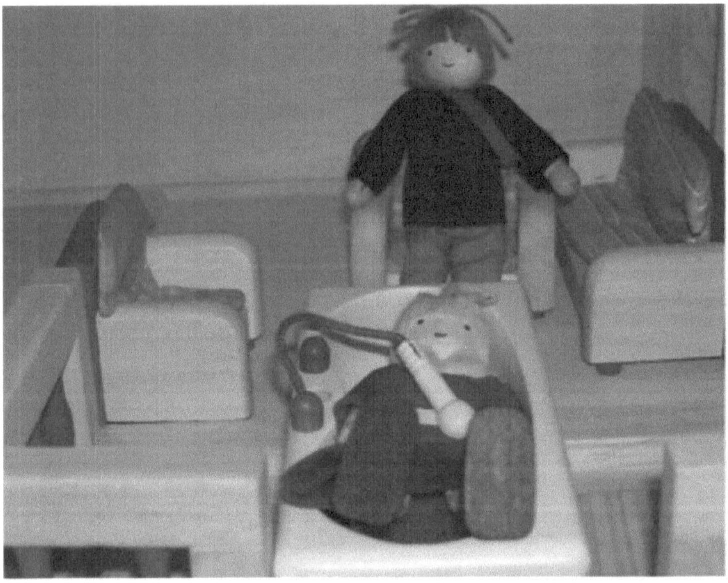

Figure 2.4 The dollhouse's bathroom is set up with a bathtub and a shower hose. The mum doll is lying in the bathtub. The dad doll is sitting at the back of the mum doll's head.

Based partly on her dad's description of their visits to her mum at the hospital, Ronia creates her own pictures and memories. The room shows how she wants to remember it with the visitor chairs and "some kind of machine" on her mum's stomach that "doesn't really work". Hugs are not part of the picture.

Ronia ends the game by saying:

It doesn't really work.
No, it doesn't, I understand.

Our conversation during the remainder of the session centres on all the illnesses that mums can get. Ronia knows many:

They can get a toothache, they can skin their knees, they can get bad backs, a cold and cancer. The worst is a cold.

I want to bring the conversation closer to her and say:

It's really no fun having a cold. But stomach cancer is usually worse because then the hospital cannot always help.
Oh, yes, you're right. I forgot about that, Ronia says.

I nod to indicate that she knows that I know that what she is saying is based on her own experiences, even if it concerns a doll mum. This makes it less frightening.

Ronia's mother fell ill shortly after Ronia's birth, it turned out, and Ronia knows that this was the case. This must have made her wonder if mothers can come down with certain illnesses because they are carrying a baby in their stomach. If so, it could be "her fault" that her mother became ill with cancer, especially cancer in the tummy (I used the word "tummy" since, to a child at this age, she feels that this is the place for babies, food and terrible diseases). I therefore lead the conversation back to the Indian mum and her baby:

The Indian baby is so little that it must have been in its mum's stomach not too long ago.
It's really adorable, says Ronia and strokes the little baby.
Yes, it's really darling. Have you seen pictures of yourself when you were so little?
I wanna a little sister. I think it's unfair that Anna was first and then I hadda be a little sister.

Yes, Anna does not need to bear any feelings of guilt as I suspect Ronia does. When her sister was in their mum's stomach, their mum did not become ill. Without really knowing if I am on track, I say:

It's never a baby's fault if its mother gets something wrong with her stomach.
No, course not, says Ronia weakly.

She sits calmly and ponders what I have said. I cannot let go of the thought of my forgetfulness and ask:

What do you think we should do about the Indian mum?
She's gone, remember?
But together we can figure out where she can be, you know.

Just because a mum is gone in reality does not mean that the thoughts about her need to go away. Ronia goes to the shelf where she previously fetched the Indian woman and finds her there.

What are those things on her? asks Ronia and gives me the Indian.

I take her in my hand and look carefully to see what Ronia means and answer:

Those are feathers. Indians usually wore feathers. They're hanging down the mum's back.
Oh, I see. I thought she had wings.
Should we pretend she has wings?
Fly away with her, fly to heaven.

I fly with the Indian mum up to the top shelf of the toy cupboard, which I let symbolize heaven. There I place her on a beautiful little pillow.

She flew away, says Ronia matter-of-factly.
Yes, she did. Do you believe she can look down and see what we're doing? I ask.
Yes, I think she probably can.

Ronia comes over and sits on the chair across from me. We look at the Indian perched high up there, and I ask:

Do you often wonder where your mum is?
No, not so much. Nicole says that people turn into angels when they die.
Oh really, does she say that?
Yes, one time when she was at church they told her that.
Do you know what an angel is?
Yes, someone with wings and a white gown and golden hair.

We round off the conversation. Ronia has said earlier that she prefers to think of her mum as she was when she was healthy and I naturally want to respect that. I ask after a pause:

How're things at school?
Pretty good. There're twenty-two kids in our class. I'm in the red group.
How're things going with your teacher? I wonder, since Ronia has been so angry with her teacher for finding out about Hanna.
She's okay. She's changed. She's better now. She's actually kinda nice.
You were afraid she'd say something about your mum. Has she done that?
Yes, but everyone does, you know.
Yes, and I understand that you don't want them to do that.

I feel great warmth for this little girl, who wants to escape from all the talk about her being motherless that meets her at every turn. However, I have the feeling that her teacher treats her just like any other child in the class and not like a poor little thing, which otherwise is a common experience for Ronia.

When the session is over she bounds down the stairs and shouts in the stairwell:

See you next Wednesday.
Yes, I'll be waiting for you then.

While I straighten up the room I think about how the Indian mum was not where she should have been and what that ended up meaning. Ronia was able to use my mistake in a way that made it into a turning point in her therapy. It was strong of her to seize the opportunity and approach the missing mother.

Hard work building up a new family

Session 7

Right before each therapy session I phone the receptionist and ask her to send Ronia up to my room. But today I am three minutes late in phoning her. When Ronia sees me, she cries out in surprise:

But where've you been? Why weren't you at home?

She believes, as do many of the younger children, that I live in the therapy room. I say:

I'm sorry I'm late. I know you don't like for me to be late. I wanted to be ready to start on time for you but it wasn't possible today. Things went wrong, and I know it's not good.

She just barely accepts my apology, and I promise not to let it happen again. I am glad that she does not demand an explanation. There is no way to tell her the truth, which is that the little patient before her made it necessary for me to do lots of cleaning up after his session. She strides into the room and stands facing me. She looks embarrassed when she shows me her new clothes and her new, flattering hairstyle. I compliment her:

Oh, how nice! Please spin around so that I can see you from the back as well.

She does as I request and I spend a good while admiring her, looking at her from different angles, and say:

You're wearing new clothes that suit you really well. The colours in your sweater look really good on you. And you have a new hairstyle, too. You look like an elegant schoolgirl. And what do you think? Do you like the way you look now? I ask.

I guess so, says Ronia, who is not used to accepting compliments.

Well, take a good look at yourself in the mirror when you get home, I encourage her, *so that you can see how perfectly that light blue sweater goes with your eyes. You look just great!*

Dad's girlfriend bought sweaters for all of us. Five sweaters. She's gonna cut all the other kids' hair too 'cause she thinks it costs too much money if we all go to a hairdresser.

Yes, you're five kids now, after all. She's done a good job of cutting your hair, and the style suits you very well.

She looks happy, sits on the chair across from me and wants us to talk. She pulls at her sweater and throws her hair back. I give her an admiring look and lead the conversation to the topic of school, since she sees that as her reason for coming to see me. We talk about how she now knows all the children in her class. It turns out that it was a stroke of good fortune when her teacher let the girl who wanted to find a friend sit beside Ronia. She tells me excitedly:

Her name's Nicole. She's really nice. She's brown and she's 'dopted. We're best friends.

Ronia talks warmly about her new friend and gives me lots of details. The way she talks indicates that her mind is more open now. It turns out that Nicole has been adopted from Colombia. Ronia seems never to have known a child before with so much and such curly hair because she is especially fascinated by Nicole's hair. Exactly as Ronia predicted, all her classmates know that she has no mother. If one person finds out, then everyone knows. It is always that way. Nicole, who seems used to having to answer questions about her origins, tells Ronia right away that she knows two people who are dead. The one is her grandmother and the other is a brother she had in Colombia. Nicole has also told Ronia that her "tummy mum" had no money for food. Nicole was therefore adopted and taken to Stockholm when she was three years old and got another mother.

So that was good, of course, Ronia says matter-of-factly when she has told me Nicole's story.
I see, so she got a new mother.

I understand between the lines that Ronia has been able to relieve her heavy heart a little bit by talking to Nicole about her mum because Nicole has asked why Ronia does not have a new mum yet. Nicole seems to be a child who thinks about life and appreciates things because she has said, "A mum's good to have." Her new mum is nice according to what Ronia has seen in the schoolyard.

Ronia is becoming more and more relaxed, partly thanks to her awareness that her dad values his own talks with me. With her dad taken care of, she can concentrate more easily on her own difficulties. Through the years Ronia has always been afraid that something would happen to her dad. She sees that his spirit is lighter, which makes her happy and reduces her anxiety. Ronia shows that she has a pent-up need to talk to someone who does not get a sorrowful look on her face as soon as Ronia opens her mouth.

At this session Ronia does not show any signs of wanting to do anything but talk, so I cautiously stay on the theme of mums. Up to this point she has approached this theme for the most part by playing with various female dolls, but now she tries to find words for her own thoughts and not only for the dolls. We work together and talk for a while about mums in general while we gradually approach her mum in particular. I want to make her mum Hanna's presence in the therapy room more concrete. Ronia needs this to happen in order to be able to create her own picture of her mum on her own terms. If she is going to be able to talk about her mum in a natural way, she herself must choose what is important for her to remember.

She has heard enough about what others think she should know. With this in mind, I say:

I'm sitting here thinking about what your mother looked like, Ronia.
Well, her hair's kinda light.
Oh, I see. It sounds like she had the same hair colour as you.

Ronia speaks in the present tense and I in the past, but I do not comment on that. I continue making small talk about her mum until Ronia shows me that it is enough for today. She does so by fetching a deck of cards and dealing them out to us. We end the hour by playing Funny Families but neither of us does especially well. Ronia shows me different cards, and we laugh at how ridiculous the figures look. The object of the game is for each of us to collect as many sets of four figures that make up a funny family as we can.

Ronia is tired, throws her cards on the table, yawns and says:

I never get a whole family. I give up.
Yes, it's hard work building up a new family, hard work for everyone, I reply.

Ronia shows clear signs of how strenuous it is and I add:

But it usually works out in the end, even though it takes lots of time and energy.
I get so awfully tired, says Ronia in the middle of yet another yawn.
Yes, I understand that. Therapy also puts a strain on you. All children think so.

When the session is over, Ronia comes to life. She is looking forward to the café where she and her dad go after therapy, just the two of them. As she breezes down the stairs, she calls out aloud to herself that she is going to choose a pastry with green icing today.

Should be forbidden for mums to die

Session 8

While she is still coming up the stairs on her way to the eighth session, Ronia pulls an envelope out of the back pocket of her new jeans. She has asked her dad to give her a picture of her mum. I watch her fumble as she opens the envelope, and it occurs to me that she has probably never before carried a photo of her mum with her. She smiles embarrassedly and reaches out to me with the photo, which has become slightly creased. I take it and notice right away that Ronia closely resembles her mum. I see her mum's medium-blonde hair and her blue eyes. While I, taking ample time and great care, look at the picture of her mother, Hanna, Ronia's gaze is glued to my face. When I have finally finished looking, I ask her if it is all right for the picture to remain lying on the table, so that we can look at it some more if we want. She nods in agreement and most likely wonders why I am not saying anything about the picture right away.

The atmosphere in the room is calm and serene. I smile at Ronia and nod affirmatively when I put the photo on the table, but I still do not say anything. I do not want to jump ahead of her with my observations about her mum. Other people have naturally told her everything, precisely everything positive that they have known about her. This is always the case. Ronia notices that I take another approach when I see the picture. We sit quietly and contemplate the picture of her mum for a long while. It warms my heart to see Ronia confident that what we are doing now can help her, even though it feels so tough. Ronia starts to dangle her legs, which is a signal that she is ready to continue. She fetches paper and crayons and starts to draw and colour. We chit-chat while she colours.

Ronia lets me understand that she wants to talk about an ordinary mum. She makes it clear that she no longer wants to think about a mum who is ill, who has no hair, cannot see and cannot walk. No, she wants to think about a healthy mum, who is out for a walk with her children, and that is precisely what she is drawing. I continue:

The first time we met, you said that you didn't want to hug your mum when she was so ill. You didn't like her to be ill. Your dad has believed that you were the one who hugged her that time, but it was Anna who hugged her. I think it was good that you told him that. His memory was wrong.

Ronia listens and goes on dangling her legs.

You were little so perhaps you thought it was horrible.
Yes, that's right. But no one understands. And it is horrible, it really is.

Ronia still uses the present tense when she speaks about her mother.

Little children always feel that way. They don't recognize their mum when they see her at the hospital. They want her to come home and for everything to be as usual again. That's what you wanted, too.

She is relieved to hear that other children also react as she did, so I continue:

Children can also get angry that their mum is dying.
It should be forbidden for mums to go and die, says Ronia after having thought about it for a while.

I could not agree more. I also think so, with all my heart, and answer:

Yes, I think so, too, absolutely!
Nicole also thinks so, she really does. She's told me so.

I realize that I have a little ally in Nicole. She and I both want to help Ronia along the way, each in our own manner.

She builds up her courage for an outburst and makes it:

Mum was really dumb in the head. It was super ridiculous of her to go and die.

Ronia laughs hysterically, and I let her vent her feelings that way for a good amount of time before I say something about my position:

It's not at all strange to feel that way. Many people do, they really do. When it comes to feelings, there's nothing that is right or wrong.

She looks a little amazed at herself for having dared to make such a strong statement as a way of testing whether she is really allowed to think this way. No one has ever spoken that way about her mum, Hanna. Ronia squeezes in another comment:

She was really wacko, my mum!

She picks up the photo and waves it around. I turn on the table lamp and suggest that we prop up the photo against it. Toward the end of the session I ask:

Maybe you didn't think your mum would be dead for such a long time?
Anna didn't either.
Children don't usually understand that it's forever. But when someone dies, she's dead forever.

Ronia is completely silent while she contemplates her response. She likes to hear that she is not alone in her thoughts but that other children also think the way she does. She is in the process of abandoning the little hope she has nourished that her mother would be able to come back against all the odds. She convinces herself by counting up various reasons why this can never happen now:

She can't come home 'cause we've moved, you know. She doesn't know where it is. It's crowded at our place, too, and we're gonna get a new baby. Now Carolina's sleeping in mum's bed. Anna and I used to believe we'd see mum lying there in her bed the next day.
She's not coming back, I say, even though I do not like what I have to say.

I repeat the same thing once again. Ronia starts to talk about "home," and now it is the new flat that she means. I have not heard anything about a new baby, and I do not know if the baby is Ronia's fantasy or reality. After all, she does think it is a nuisance to be the youngest.

Would you like to have a little brother or sister?
But it's true; we're gonna get a new baby. I know that.
Okay, I see.

I ask what Ronia thinks we should do with the picture of her mum, but she does not really know. I therefore suggest that we can keep it in a safe place with me. Whenever we meet we can prop the picture up against the table lamp and turn on the lamp. That way we can look at Hanna whenever we want. Ronia brightens up and goes along with my suggestion. I remind her that we are going to meet two more times, which she is keeping track of on her own. We talk about how things will be when therapy ends. I mention that she has grown during the time that I have known her. Unlike many children, Ronia does not ask for a chance to come more than ten times. She has shown right from the start that the number ten is almost sacred for her. In preparation for the two remaining sessions, I must remember to place the Indian mum on the top shelf, which has now become established as her place, and put the photo of Ronia's mum on the table.

My children, your children and our child

Discussion with Ronia's dad

Peter's mind is occupied with the makeover of their flat, and he tells me that he is employing workmen for the first time. He is an electrician himself and knows almost all there is to know when it comes to building. But they have to make the flat liveable as soon as possible, and he does not have enough time to do it himself. Of course, he has a hard time forcing himself not to interfere with the workmen in their work. He has now completed two months of work at his new job in Stockholm, and he likes the friendly atmosphere there.

Peter observes that he has also gone through a lot that has been new for him since he left everything behind and moved to Stockholm. He had believed that he had worked himself through the loss of his wife, but everything that has happened with Ronia has evoked his feelings of loss and grief once more. He thinks a lot about how his life has been and how the future is going to be, everything hits him at the same time. Carolina leaves him alone and gives him space for his thoughts. She understands him since she has gone through the same process herself. I talk about how it is also a matter of great significance to change one's identity, from having been a widower and a father alone with two children to taking up house with one's fiancée and five children. Peter is well aware that things are not going to be easy, but he feels it is worth whatever sacrifices it takes.

He tells me that things are going better for Ronia at school. Her new friend Nicole sometimes comes to their place for a play date. She appreciates the lively mix of building material and many children, since she lives alone with her mum. Ronia's teacher has said that she enjoys school now but that she has a number of gaps in her knowledge. It is undoubtedly because everyone has been completely focused on helping Anna and Ronia through their grief and therefore normal knowledge acquisition has had to wait. We talk about how children must feel well psychically in order to be able to learn new things and how Ronia now feels better. I suggest that Peter should ask his daughter what she would like to learn from her dad. I am sure there is something she notices that her peers know but that she does not.

It has occurred to Peter only recently that Ronia has not had anyone to talk to about her mum earlier. She has not been able to express her loss to her grandma, who has taken care of her on many occasions. She has tried, but she sees that she is making her grandma sad. Her grandma has said that they can talk about it later but then Ronia has not wanted to. It has been hard for grandmother and granddaughter to get together in a talk about Hanna, Ronia's mother and grandma's daughter. Our talk continues with Peter's mentioning Ronia's new clothes and new hairstyle. Carolina does not think the child has enough clothes.

Peter says apologetically that Ronia's clothes have always been a tricky subject. She has never cared about clothes in the same way as Anna always has. When he goes shopping with Anna, she knows what she wants, but Ronia never does. We talk about how it is getting more and more important to involve Ronia in decisions about how she looks. Of course she wants to be treated as a schoolgirl and not a little child any longer. Peter says that he has also noticed how Ronia is more readily looked upon as a poor little thing if she is uncombed and wearing clothes that look slept in. He says he is ashamed but grateful that both Carolina and I have brought this issue to his attention.

Peter says that Ronia now feels better than he does and thus they are out of step in the other direction. He has not yet recovered from the shock he experienced when he realized Ronia was suffering so much without his understanding what was going on. In addition, everything has gone so fast recently, with his newly found love for Carolina and the new family. She is pregnant. They had not planned this baby, but they want to have a child together. Since Carolina is forty-two years old they would not have been able to wait especially long anyway. Peter is just afraid that with a new baby everything is going to be too burdensome for Carolina. How will it work out? It must work out. Peter wants to feel the same joyful anticipation as he did with Anna and Ronia. He wonders when he is going to tell the children about the baby.

I tell him that Ronia has already told me the news. Peter stares at me and looks like he thinks he has not heard me correctly. He is dumbstruck out of pure surprise. How does she know that? Yes, Ronia is well attuned to the emotional signals of other people. Children in her situation can need to assure themselves that nothing unforeseen is going to happen. The surest means to this end is to learn quickly to read others' facial expressions and emotional signals. I guide the conversation to touch on Peter's belief that the entire situation has been less difficult for Anna since she has memories of her mother. My understanding is instead that it has been easier to help Anna because she is clearer and quicker at expressing her feelings than Ronia is. We talk about how it has been important for him to see that his daughters preserve their memories of their mother. Peter has noticed that Ronia has been a little quieter about her mum recently. He realizes the importance of giving Ronia a chance to form her own memory images of her mum. He has simply not thought of this earlier.

Dad's girlfriend has changed for the better

Session 9

When Ronia arrives for her second to last session, I have done everything right. The Indian woman is out on the shelf, and the photo of Ronia's mum is on the table. She glances at the clock and says that our session begins when the little hand points to two. When she sees that everything is in order, she goes up to the photo of her mum and props it up against the shining table lamp. Ronia gets to decide when we should look at the photo and she wants us to do so right away. I guide the conversation to focus on the qualities her mum had that can be important for a seven-year-old to know about. We chat about her mum, and I say:

Do you know what your mum's favourite colour was?
She wears blue clothes a lot of the time.
She is wearing a blue sweater in the picture, I say matter-of-factly.

Ronia twists and turns the picture and runs her fingers over her mum's sweater when we talk about it.

You also look very good in blue, Ronia. Your blue eyes are even prettier when there's blue in your sweater. Your hair and eyes are the same colour as your mum's were.
How do you know?
I see it when I look at you and at the picture of your mum.
You do? Well, okay.
Do you think you got your colours from her?
Well, maybe.
I think so because your dad has brown hair and brown eyes. Your mum didn't have those colours.

I speak in the past tense and do not comment on how she continues to use the present. I guess that she does not speak in the past tense about her mum because she is not used to doing so yet. I continue to talk and ask:

Do you know what your mum's favourite food was?
She likes meatballs, I know that. I do too. Yummy. Delicious. Grandma usually makes meatballs when she's at our place.
Oh, I see. Then you had the same taste, your mum and you. You both probably got it from your grandma.
How do you know?
Well, that's the way it usually is.

I want to bring up things that help Ronia to build up a history of her own about her mum. She needs to do so on her own terms and not based on memories that others ascribe to her. I mention to Ronia that no children have true memories from the time they were two years old. She has indicated earlier that she is eager to hear about how things are for other children who have a dead mum, so I tell her:

I know several children who had a mum who died when they were little.
What're their names?

I say some names in order to make the conversation more concrete.

Louis, Selma, Isaac, Amanda, Emma and Anna.

She wants to hear more about these children. I tell her about common ways of reacting and say that not one of these children who was two years old when his or her mum died can have true memories of that mum. Ronia is surprised that she is not alone in thinking as she does and that there are so many other children with the same experiences. She counts on her fingers to see how many names I mentioned. She has never met anyone, except of course Nicole, who does not have her real mum but instead someone else she calls mum. Ronia wants to talk some more about her mum.

She could sing, dad told me.
Do you like to sing?
My teacher says that I can "carry a tune". I asked her what that means, and she said it means you can sing.
Then you also get that from your mum. Parents can pass on a good singing voice to their children. It's fun to sing.

Now Ronia is engaged in the conversation and wants to add more:

Mum was the one who wanted to name me Ronia. I don't know anyone else named Ronia. Dad decided that Anna should be named Anna.
Maybe your mum chose the name Ronia because she was thinking of the children in Astrid Lindgren's stories. One of them is named Ronia. Astrid's storybook children come out on top, come rain or shine, even if they get into tough situations. Things always work out for them in the end.

After a while I continue:

You're sitting there thinking about something.
I've seen the film about Ronia the robber's daughter.

She tells me about the film with her namesake and other films of Astrid Lindgren's stories that she has seen many times. Her favourites are the films about Ronia the robber's daughter and about Pippi Longstocking.

It feels as though Ronia's mum is here with us in the room, which indicates that Ronia is in the process of creating her own image of her mum. She no longer needs to keep her an arm's length away, neither in her thoughts nor in her feelings. When a dead parent's presence can be felt in the air, it indicates that the grieving process has moved forward. Ronia also begins to speak of her mother in the past tense.

I state matter-of-factly that we have only one session left. She says that she knows this, but I still want to talk about the approaching conclusion. We compare how things were when she came in the beginning and was angry, frightened and unhappy versus how she feels now. It was not easy for her at that point, before she could know how everything new was going to turn out and before she could know that lots of things would get better. We talk about school and her best friend. She mentions that her teacher and Carolina have both changed for the better.

To make the conclusion of our therapy sessions more concrete, we talk about what we are going to do on Wednesday afternoons when we will no longer be meeting. Ronia says that she is going to start playing football with some girls in her class. She wants to try new things so she can see what she likes best. She has never played football. I suggest that we end our next session, which is the last one, by meeting together all three of us, Ronia, her dad and I. Before I have completed my suggestion she objects and says that she and I are meant to meet ten times, just the two of us. She is not prepared to give up one single minute. I explain that we can add fifteen minutes to our last meeting. That way the three of us can meet after Ronia's therapy time is over. When she understands my idea in full, she goes along with it.

When there are several minutes left of this eventful session, Ronia goes to the dollhouse and looks at the mess there. She sorts out the dolls and finds a tiny computer, a skateboard, a shower with a shower curtain and a bicycle. She arranges all of these things in one of the rooms beside a boy doll with a cap on. Does this possibly indicate that she has become curious about Carolina's three sons and their things? The colours of their things differ completely from those of Anna and Ronia. Now she creates order in the dollhouse. The room with the mum in the bathtub remains untouched.

Next time I'm gonna clean up some more so they can live there.
Yes, it's going to be our last time, the last time of all.

Clean up and move in, divide up the space, both physically and psychically – these are the present concerns of her newly formed family.

Time is up. Ronia jumps into her new shoes that she has taken off and waves a kiss at her dead mum in the picture on the table. This comes 100 percent spontaneously from Ronia herself and looks genuine. She brings her hand to her mouth and giggles as though she has surprised herself. As a goodbye to me she thrusts her fist up into the air before she lies down on her stomach on the stair rail and zooms down. Ronia has become significantly more robust and lively. As she coasts down the rail she looks like a seven-year-old who thinks it is exciting to try new things.

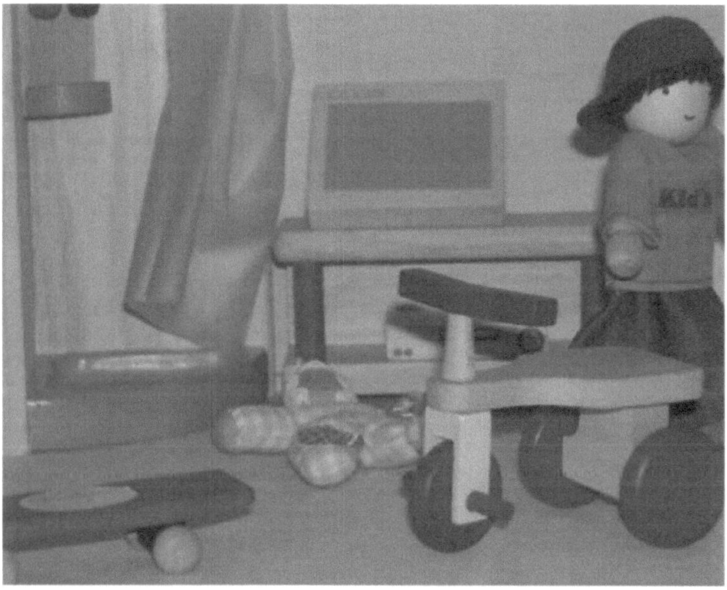

Figure 2.5 Yet another room in the dollhouse is set up with furniture. There is just the right amount of tidiness and order when the most important items are put into place. These are a skateboard, a computer, a bicycle and a shower.

Ronia shows that she is taking part in the furnishing of her new home. She sorts things out, cleans up, distributes things and moves in. Two children are to share a room.

Why didn't anyone tell me she'd be dead so long?

Session 10

When Ronia comes to her final session, she strides into the room with decisive steps. She takes the mum picture from the table, goes over to the dollhouse and puts the picture on a chair beside her. She pays no attention to the Indian mum. She does not need to go a roundabout way via her now that she has established a good way of taking in her own mum. She talks to herself while she puts everything in order in the dollhouse. She mumbles:

There's no order here. Everything's out of place. Oh dear, what a mess! Where's everyone actually 'sposed to live? There's not enough room for everyone.

She counts all the dolls several times before she gets it right. Sometimes she rattles off numbers faster than she has time to point her finger at each doll. She counts far beyond ten of them, takes away the grandmother and grandfather dolls and says:

They gotta live in their own house. Only some of the dolls are gonna live here.

A couple of other dolls do not get to stay in the house either. She arranges all the furniture and places the remaining dolls in the different rooms. The dolls get to try various chairs and beds but cannot agree on which ones of them are going to share a room with each other. She tries out ideas, changes her mind and rearranges things. This is no easy task, and it does not get easier when she is ready to distribute the computer, the skateboard, the bicycle, the toilet seats and the shower. All of the dolls want to have certain precise things but they have to share because there is, for example, only one computer. The dollhouse gets crowded, but she solves this problem by letting two of the dolls sleep on the balcony. In compensation they are given some little flowers. At last all the dolls are in place, and she says:

Now it's really time to say enough is enough.

Figure 2.6 The entire dollhouse is now in order and ready for moving in. After some minor arguing between the dolls, everyone is in place at last.

Ronia clearly shows that she is in the process of making herself at home with her new family. All family members have been given their fair share of what they need, which bodes well for the future.

I admire Ronia for the way she shows via the dollhouse that she is involving herself in the planning for a large family with all her heart and soul. She is going to express her opinions there at home and no longer leave it to the others to decide things for her. She gives me a distinct feeling that she is busy making herself at home in the new flat. When the dollhouse has received the final touches, she takes the mum picture with her, throws herself on the couch, lies on her back and takes a long look at her mum. Ronia wants us to repeat what we talked about at the last session, so we take up Ronia's name, her singing voice, her blue eyes and medium-blonde hair, her preference for meatballs and other qualities that have been passed on to her by her mum.

When we have finished talking, Ronia looks at me and asks:

Why didn't anyone tell me she'd be dead so long? No one ever told me that.

They thought you knew. But how could you know when no one ever told you? We don't just know things on our own when we're young.

It was really stupid that they didn't tell me.

Yes, it was, but even grown-ups have a hard time really understanding that someone is dead forever.

How long will she be dead? Ronia asks, but it sounds mostly like a rhetorical question, just to be sure.

When someone dies, it's forever. A mum who's dead isn't coming back. It's always like that.

Yes, that's what I thought, Ronia sighs.

But now you know many things about your mum. You know what things about yourself come from her. All of this will stay in your heart. In our hearts we cherish things that are important and good and that we never want to forget.

I pat her gently on her chest as she lies there on the couch to show her where her heart is. She wants me to keep my hand there, so I sit for a good while beside her and chat about her heart and about how she can save whatever she wishes to save inside there. The choice is hers, and that choice does not include any memory of hugging her mum that final time. For Ronia it is more important to think of her mum's best dish and her favourite colours and of the fact that she has inherited her mum's eye and hair colour.

All of those things are there in your heart whenever you think about your mum Hanna. Other people want to remember other things in their hearts when they think about Hanna. This decision is up to each and every one of you.

With that final hug, the one that never took place, in mind, I add:

Your dad believed earlier that you were the one who hugged your mum that time, but it wasn't you. You couldn't do that. You were so little.

I didn't reach up to the bed.
No, exactly, the bed was too high so you couldn't reach. And maybe you were a bit frightened as well. All children get scared if their mums are ill. But you and your mum hugged each other many other times.

To prevent Ronia from fantasizing further about the consequences of that absent final hug, I say:

No one's going to be punished for not being able to give a hug. No child and no adult.
Oh, is that so? Well, I guess that's good anyhow.

I repeat that I know what I am saying is true. Ronia listens carefully until she thinks it is enough. She looks into the dollhouse, thinks about Carolina and fools around with a little baby doll. She sounds softer in tone when she says:

Anna calls Carolina by the name Karolinska.

She giggles, and I understand that she and her sister have tested every imaginable name for their stepmother, even this one, Karolinska, the name of the world-renowned Swedish research and medical complex. She laughs so forcefully that I cannot hear all the names they have come up with. Most names sound like abusive nicknames they have been compelled to get out of their heads before they could agree to call her Caro, a common nickname for Carolina.

What do the boys call your dad? I wonder.
Peter, of course, Ronia answers indignantly.

It apparently has not occurred to her that the boys might like to have a part of Peter as their dad.

I think of the Karolinska Hospital in Stockholm and its maternity ward, and I wonder how sure Ronia is that Carolina is not going to disappear when she goes to that hospital to give birth to the new baby. Ronia's experience of hospitals is that mums become ill when they go there to give birth and never get well again. I therefore sustain these themes throughout the last part of the session: mums, Carolina, baby and hospital.

Against her will, Ronia is beginning to like Carolina, so I ask:

What do you think will happen in case you start liking Carolina?
Aw, she's pretty nice sometimes, but actually she's a pain in the neck.

We talk about what can happen just in case she decides Carolina is nice. We conclude that nothing bad can come out of that. No one is going to die. Carolina is healthy, so she will not become ill after she has had the baby. She is going to come home from the hospital with a little sister or brother. Ronia is not really clear yet over the fact that her own dad is going to be the baby's dad. But she has time to get used to the idea.

Ronia lets various fantasies come to the surface and tests ambivalent feelings about what could happen if she should chance to call Caro "mum" some time.

The boys call out "mum" all the time but sometimes they say "mummy", Ronia sniggers.

I can guess that Caro has a tough job ahead of her as mum, stepmum and mummy. I want us to talk about things that are good about her.

What did you mean when you said that Caro is pretty nice sometimes?
Well, she gives us each a turn to choose what we wanna have for dinner.

Ronia tells me about different dishes that the children choose, and she is pleasantly surprised that the boys have almost the same favourites as she and Anna do. She has chosen meatballs for her dinner.

How do they taste?
Actually pretty good, answers Ronia and does not look the least bit doubtful.

Our therapy session is over, and Ronia slides down all the stair rails and fetches Peter. When they come up she is pulling her dad by the hand. She is excited and wants to show him the dollhouse. He bends down and looks inside it while I help Ronia tell him how she has been working with dividing up everything fairly. Her dad understands and says that the flat is supposed to be completely ready this week. He is looking forward to how wonderful it will be when everything is in place and everyone can get settled. He looks at Ronia and says:

I didn't know that I have such a clever girl. You've adjusted yourself to all the new things faster than I have. You've said you want to learn to swim and we've talked about that. We're going to make it happen when summer comes. You also want to learn to tell time. We're going to buy you a watch today after we've been to the café.

We talk about the café visits, which both of them have enjoyed. They have had time to talk and have gotten closer to each other.

My cell phone's been turned off, says Peter and flashes me a loaded, self-ironic grin.
Good, keep on letting it be that way when you're having an important conversation and don't want to be disturbed.
Aye, aye, madam captain, Peter says and gives a hint of a salute.

Now it is my turn to bear the brunt of the joke, and I start to laugh. Peter and Ronia laugh as well.

Your good sense of humour's going to serve you well now when you have so many kids around you, soon half a dozen, I say.

Yes, believe me, I've already noticed that. Humour makes things easier with teenagers. I could be funny in the old days. Now my talent seems to have come back, it really has. By the way, the baby we're expecting is a girl. Ronia thinks girls are best. I think so as well, says Peter and pats Ronia on the head.
Ronia enjoys life more now and feels good, I say.

Peter lets Ronia understand how glad and thankful he is for that.

A stone has been lifted from here, he says, and gestures toward his chest.
Do you mean your heart? Ronia inserts.
Yes, Ronia, you're my heart, says her dad and embraces his daughter.
But what about Caro?

Peter is stuck so I give him a helping hand by saying:

But Anna and you were in there first.

Peter agrees and I continue:

That's the way it is. You've always got your children and your mum and dad in your heart. They always have their place there, right Ronia?

She answers by looking pleased. She smiles, squeezes herself down into Peter's armchair and leans closely against him.

They went to see Ronia's teacher for a progress report yesterday. Together they tell me what she said. Ronia enjoys school and has made more friends, even though Nicole is the one she hangs out with the most. Her teacher thinks the two girls are good for each other. She also says that Ronia needs to work on certain things. General knowledge, Peter explains, and thinks it was a good thing for him to hear.

It's never occurred to me that a seven-year-old needs to have general knowledge, but I realize it's true when I actually think about it. Ronia has never played around on computers, which all of the kids in her class have done. We're going to do something about that as well and get one more computer.

I end the therapy by saying to Ronia:

It's been a real pleasure for me to get to know you and your dad. Things are going to work out for you, Ronia, because you're a fighter. I've seen that in you. Now you know what you want and that's great!

I remind them that I am going to contact them in six months to hear how things are going. Peter thinks this is reassuring and says:

I've become aware of many things about Ronia, yes, and, frankly, about myself as well.

Peter takes a hearty grip and shakes my hand, thanking me for the help they have received. Ronia gives me a hug, and before we say goodbye I pat her meaningfully on her chest. She understands that I am reminding her about her heart and its authentic content. She laughs and pretends that I am tickling her. We wave at each other as they go down the stairs. Peter is holding the picture of mum in his hand and is asking Ronia what kind of watch she wants. I do not hear her answer but I see from her unmistakable gesturing that she is showing her dad what she wants it to look like.

Six months later

Ronia has taken her own initiative to tell her teacher about her mum and has shown her the picture of Hanna. Whenever she makes new friends she tells them that her mum is dead and that she, Ronia, lives with her dad and Carolina and their children, which number six in total. The addition to the family is a little baby girl, who was born three months ago. Ronia and Carolina's oldest son are the ones who are fondest of their little sister. They joke about whose sister she is the most.

The anger that Ronia had as a protective shield when I first met her has disappeared rather quickly and has not come back. Even when I saw it back then it struck me as somewhat loosely attached. Ronia has never been an aggressive child. She has become much more outspoken and less withdrawn. Peter says that things have gone better than he had dared to hope. Ronia never says "dad's girlfriend" these days but rather calls Carolina by her nickname Caro. She has even let down her guard sometimes and called out "mum" to her. The two of them have spoken to each other about this issue, and Carolina thinks that Ronia should try different things until she finds out what feels right. She has said that she will respond no matter what Ronia chooses to call her. Ronia has no complaints at all about Carolina's meatballs. She now thinks that "second best" is good enough, which shows that she has come a long way in working through the great loss she has suffered. I am happy to hear that she can now accept such things from another woman, as she cannot get from her mum.

When a parent dies

Why is it important for children to get help in working through grief reactions? We can understand that it is necessary when we talk to older people who have lost a parent through death when they were children. They tell us that it was devastating to lose a parent, but the hardest thing to get over was that no one ever spoke to them about the deceased. As children they felt lonely and abandoned in their grief and felt that no one cared about them or the deceased parent. If someone had just spoken to them, their loss would have been less painful. They mean that it would also have left fewer scars in their soul. It is these scars that have played the greatest role for various difficulties that have arisen during their childhood and adolescence. However, the conventional wisdom has earlier been that we should not remind children about those loved ones who have died. In that way they would forget faster. But a child cannot stop missing a parent whose care she would have needed for still more years to come.

Children who experience a death in the family obviously need lots of support, consolation, security and practical help. Together with adults who are calm and secure and who first and foremost have the capacity to listen, but who can also talk comfortingly, most children manage to get through something as extremely difficult as a parent's death. In such a vulnerable situation, every child struggles to take command in the way that is possible for that particular child at that particular time. A child's own healing capacity is strong and should never be underestimated. However, for healing to take place, a child must find a way to express her inconceivable and overpowering feelings. For various reasons all children are not able to do so to a full extent but instead need extra help.

When, then, does a child need professional psychological help? Every child is unique in her grief, and ways of expressing grief are as many as there are children. In a severely stricken family, a little child becomes the automatic life nerve. All of the relatives' will to live circles around the child, who can have a hard time taking in all of this well-intended but sorrowful attention. If these feelings become too strong, they can contribute to the child's remaining a poor little thing who makes other people unhappy as soon as she appears. We need to be on the lookout for signs that a child needs help. We see one such sign when the child continues to evoke strong feelings of pity in others even a long time after the parent's death. If the child is stuck in the role of a poor little thing and, without understanding it, sends out "feel-sorry-for-me" signals, something must be done to help her come out of this belittling role. To be treated as a poor little motherless thing over a long period of time, as Ronia has experienced, is disastrous. No one expects or demands especially much of a poor pitiful little thing.

In such cases crisis therapy for the child and supportive discussions for the parent can be of good help. In therapy the child gets a chance to meet a professional person who does not become unhappy the same minute the child opens her mouth and who has met many other children in the same situation. When a considerable amount of time has passed, the surviving parent often harbours unrealistic feelings of guilt for having failed to help the child get through her grief. The mum or dad then needs support in order to realize that she or he has done the best that was humanly possible in an extremely difficult situation.

Most children express their grief in a way that is understandable for the adults around them. They show their despair and bewilderment through different reactions. They cry, scream, become listless, cause trouble or have emotional outbursts. Children who show clear reactions, whatever they may be, are easier to help. People who are close to them understand that all the reactions are tied to the death of the loved one. In contrast, it can be harder to give adequate help to children who have a tough time showing what they feel. They withdraw more into themselves and make the people around them feel unsure. When children do not react as expected, people do not know how to approach them, and many are afraid of doing or saying something wrong. Children in these cases need professional help.

It can also be difficult to gauge a child's psychic state if she is in the midst of an intense developmental phase at the time of a parent's death. The impetus within the child to go forward is so strong that, in spite of the catastrophe, she continues to learn new skills. From the outside it may look as though her development is undisturbed and as though she is not suffering. The child's capacity temporarily exceeds the otherwise overwhelming feelings that she bears inside but is unable to show. People then often believe that the child does not understand what has happened or has already "got over it". If people are not aware that something else is going on inside the child, she will have no one with whom to share her feelings. Un-worked-through grief reactions can reappear in these children at later times in life when something especially stressful occurs. Adults close to them often need to seek psychological help on their behalf when they face a significant change, such as a school start, a move to another home or the entrance of a new partner into the family.

It is important to be on the alert to see if children, when they get older, are unable to cope with situations that entail changes or some form of leave-taking. Major difficulties in dealing with changes can indicate that a child has taken an untenable role in the family. Ronia had accepted the story that she had memories of her mother, but she knew these memories were not true ones and they prevented her from creating her own inner images and true memories. It can be difficult for a person close to the child to help her break such a pattern. With a therapist, the child gets a chance to find her role in the new family in her own way and to create memory images of the deceased parent on her own terms.

It is impossible for little children to understand that a parent has disappeared forever, since fantasy and reality exist side by side in their magical fantasy world. The dead person lives on in their fantasy as if nothing has happened, and in reality he or she is gone. The child sees nothing strange or contradictory about this. In therapy the child can be given a chance to use her fantasy as a gateway to a gradual acceptance of reality. Ronia showed that she was capable of this step when she gathered up her courage several years after her mother had died and asked her therapist how long her mother would actually be dead.

In crisis therapy the child is given her own undisturbed psychological space with a trusting atmosphere and a steady, secure rhythm. These factors are essential since the rhythm in the child's own everyday life has been shattered. The child gets a chance to work at her own pace. Nothing has to be explained or answered for by the child as would be the case in pedagogical situations. The work takes place instead on the psychological plane. Children can present thoughts and feelings that occupy them but which in other contexts can be seen as inappropriate or even rude. Feelings are not met with labels of right or wrong when a child goes to therapy.

Children in Ronia's situation can receive excellent help. It is never too late to begin a psychotherapeutic treatment, even if several years have passed since the death occurred. The focus in therapy is the same, regardless of whether a short or a long period of time has elapsed, namely, to give the child an opportunity to work through feelings that have arisen subsequent to the death of the parent as well as through reactions to a changed life situation. In crisis therapy children like Ronia get help so that they want to dare to adjust to their new life. Part of this adjustment is the ability to accept from another adult, perhaps the surviving parent's new partner, such things as cannot be provided by the deceased parent.

3 Children who feel second-rate make others feel the same way

A psychologist receives supervision for her therapy with ten-year-old Olga

Adopted girl with heavy baggage

A young psychologist named Jenny calls on me to give her supervision in her work with a patient who has started short-term therapy with her. The patient is a ten-year-old girl who has been adopted from Russia. Jenny tells me in a sad tone about her difficulties in communicating with this patient, who so greatly needs her help. Jenny does not recognize this child's reaction when she thinks back over her work with other children. They normally do not have a problem trusting Jenny. But Jenny does not know how to approach this girl who does not want to have her as a therapist.

The girl's name is Olga, and I receive a short description of her difficulties. She feels lonely and unhappy, does not have any friends and is not doing well in school. She was adopted from Moscow when she was five years old and has thus lived as long in Sweden as she has in Russia. Jenny mentions a circumstance which has made the work harder. About six months ago Olga started psychotherapy with another psychologist, Gudrun. She met with her three times, after which the treatment was interrupted. The reasons come up later in the present description. Jenny is thus Olga's second psychotherapist, and she feels lost as to how she should relate to the girl, who would rather be in therapy with Gudrun. Not with Jenny.

I suggest that Jenny come to see me for four supervision sessions so that I can help her understand Olga better and find ways of approaching her. Creating a relationship of trust with a child who perhaps has not experienced enough security early in life is not an easy task for a psychologist who does not have that much experience in the profession. It requires an ability to "listen behind" things that the child is saying. The therapist must also be resilient and not let herself lose her composure because of things the child might come up with. It is important that younger colleagues get the support they need in the form of supervision when they start conducting psychotherapeutic work. I already got to know Jenny when she was doing her psychology training, so I know her to be a wise and warm person who takes her work seriously. Since the work can be emotionally draining, even colleagues with considerably more years in the profession than Jenny sometimes need to receive supervision.

I describe here Jenny's and my mutual work to make Olga's psychotherapy as efficient as possible. The narrative is written from my perspective as a supervisor and is based on Jenny's and my four meetings. In consultation with Jenny I have chosen different themes from our discussions that elucidate what takes place when a psychologist meets her supervisor. The patient continues seeing her psychologist as usual and does not meet the supervisor. Examples from Olga's therapy sessions are given in the narrative in the way that Jenny tells them to me. Short vignettes about how Olga's parents think and feel are also presented. In preparation for the supervision sessions Jenny asks me to partake of some notes on Olga's background. I also read a short account from the journal for the discontinued therapy with Gudrun. It is necessary not only for the psychotherapist to know the adopted child's background, but also for the supervisor. Equipped with this knowledge, they can both view the problems against the backdrop of what the child experienced in the early years. A summary of everything I read will open the narrative.

When Olga's parents sought psychological help for their adopted daughter, they explained that she had become devastated when a neighbour girl moved. Olga was unhappy, did not always have enough energy to go to school and had fallen behind on her schoolwork. She complained about stomach aches and did not sleep well. The parents could not sleep either and were exhausted. The girl could not accept the fact that her only friend had moved, even though four months had passed. Her teacher had told the parents that Olga could achieve much more if she could only improve her concentration. But that is exactly what she could not do, her mum explained. There were too many thoughts swirling around in her mind.

Olga's teachers were puzzled at her inability to handle her schoolwork. She was given a chance to take an aptitude test with the school psychologist. According to her dad she had done "pretty well". Olga had also started thinking lately about the fact that she was adopted and had at one point said that she "regretted the whole thing". Olga had crying attacks at home and no one knew why, least of all Olga. Sometimes she complained that no one liked her and that, of course, made the parents unhappy, because they really loved their daughter and her younger brother. They do not mention anything about any problems between the siblings.

We know the following about Olga's early life history. Olga was adopted by her Swedish parents from an orphanage together with her half-brother who at that time was just three years old. The children have the same biological mother. In the adoption papers it says the mother was already addicted to drugs and alcohol before the children were born. A biological father is not mentioned anywhere. The family lived under difficult social circumstances, and the children were taken into custody by the social services and placed in an orphanage. Olga was then three years old and her younger brother was one year old, and they lived at the orphanage for two years. As the biological mother was not heard from, a court decided that the children could be put up for international adoption.

In Olga's adoption papers it says she was in bad condition when she arrived at the orphanage. She was somewhat undernourished, under-stimulated, spoke Russian poorly for her age and had marks from rat bites on one leg. The younger brother was in better shape. It seemed that Olga had been taking care of him despite the fact that she was only three years old. There had been a discussion about whether a woman staff member at the orphanage would get to have Olga live with her at her house as a foster child. The woman's wish had been declined as it was considered better for the siblings, who were so close, to grow up together. The woman could only take one child and had grown fond of Olga.

The adoptive parents said it was not possible to talk to Olga about her background, but they suspected she had gone through difficult experiences in her past. It was easier to talk to the little brother about that fact that he comes from Russia. Olga "does not remember" anything about her life there. The parents say they often talk about things they know about Russia. When there are sporting events on TV and Russia wins some match, the parents point that out, but that kind of thing never interests Olga. Her little brother, in contrast, always roots for the same team as his dad, which is usually the Russian team.

Olga's parents were prepared that it would be a difficult task to accept a sibling pair and not just one child as was first planned. Even though they could never have anticipated how draining it would be for all four of them, the adjustment has gone fairly well. In the beginning Olga disliked everything Russian and she disliked everything Swedish even more. Midsummer and Christmas were "just ridiculous". Now, however, she enjoys these and other holidays. It has taken Olga longer than her little brother to learn Swedish.

Children in Sweden attend preschool until they are six years old, at which time there is a preparatory year called "preschool class," which they attend prior to their real school start at age seven. At the recommendation of the preschool personnel, Olga got two years in the preschool class, which turned out to be beneficial for her. During the extra year Olga developed significantly, became more proficient at Swedish and started feeling more at home in her family.

Both parents thought it was difficult to help their daughter when her friend moved away. They were perplexed by her strong reactions. They could not reach her. Her dad worried and said, "She is starting to slide out of our hands." Her mum cried and was unhappy and felt she was failing as a mother since she could not understand her child. When Olga could not sleep at night, the parents could not sleep either. They were exhausted from their sleep deprivation. They wished their daughter would get a chance to go to a psychologist to talk about all the things that weighed her down and to work through her difficult experiences in early life. The parents also asked to talk to someone who had experience with children who were adopted when they were a little older, around five years of age or maybe even in the first or second year of school. They got to meet with a psychologist by the name of Ingegerd.

When I have gone through the notes about Olga and her life history, I continue reading about the way she started and hastily interrupted her therapy with her first psychotherapist, Gudrun, who is well known to me and others for her skill in working with adopted children. When Olga was about to start her therapy with

Gudrun, there was an intense discussion at Gudrun's place of work about a reorganization that was going to be implemented. It was difficult to anticipate what this might mean for Gudrun's work situation. She did, however, agree with Olga's parents to meet with the child once a week for time-limited, short-term psychotherapy during a period of a little over three months for a total of twelve sessions. Gudrun had been promised that during this period there would be no changes in her work situation.

Olga started her therapy, and Gudrun soon noticed that Olga had difficulties talking about her current problems and her background. She did not like being asked questions. Gudrun encouraged her, therefore, to "talk" through drawing, clay work and painting as well as by building in the sand tray and playing in a dollhouse. Olga appreciated getting to express herself in these various ways and did not view it as childish, which some ten-year-olds would do. From what Olga showed through play, Gudrun understood that the child had confusing experiences from her first years, which she could not describe with words.

After a few visits Gudrun noticed that Olga started to like coming to see her. Searching for words, Olga started saying that she was sad because her friend had moved away from her. And since the friend was so stupid for doing a thing like that, Olga did not want to talk to her on the phone. Gudrun understood that she felt left behind and abandoned. It was not easy for Olga to express herself, but it became a little easier with Gudrun's support. She expressed negative thoughts about herself and could not say anything positive. Gudrun saw that Olga had a weak sense of self and low self-esteem.

When Olga had been to therapy three times Gudrun was offered early retirement as a result of the reorganization. She planned to wrap up her work in the next three months. The parents, who had overheard discussions in the waiting room about personnel changes, became worried and asked Gudrun what was going on. She told them how it was, but pointed out that this would not affect their agreement regarding their daughter's therapy. Gudrun would finish the therapy with Olga and several other children before retiring.

However, after Olga heard that Gudrun was going to leave the treatment facility, she refused to return to therapy. She felt abandoned by Gudrun even though she was not going to be abandoned at all. The mere thought of a break-up and farewell gave Olga anxiety. The parents felt helpless and were unable to convince their daughter to come at least for one last session, which is what Gudrun wanted. Summer was drawing near, and Gudrun did not succeed, despite serious effort, to get in contact with Olga. So, Gudrun wrote a card to her with a farewell message. I continue to read the account in the journal where Gudrun summarizes her meetings with Olga:

> It has become apparent that Olga has a low self-esteem and does not seem to know what she is capable of. A dear friend has moved and Olga's strong reactions to the move indicate that she suffers from separation anxiety. From this perspective it is particularly unfortunate that her therapy has not been able to go on. Olga gives the impression that she's feeling lonely and abandoned despite the love and care her adoptive parents give her. She is unhappy,

experiences herself as being bad at everything and does not have the ability to seek out other children. Olga has a hard time understanding and accepting her adoption history, but is also at an age when adoptive children usually start thinking about their origins. Her first years of life were presumably difficult. It has been documented that Olga had rat bites. The parents are encouraged to seek help again should Olga's psychic problems persist.

Considering Olga's difficult background and need of more psychological help Gudrun has pointed out that Olga's abrupt discontinuation is not because the child is incapable of benefiting from psychotherapeutic treatment. She stresses instead that the reorganization was handled in a manner that did not adequately consider vulnerable young patients. This is where Olga fell through the cracks.

Gudrun has also left a reminder note in the journal where she has written that Olga kept mumbling the same few Russian words. Nobody had understood them. Olga has also not made any attempts to translate them. Gudrun has written them down phonetically. She had a feeling they might convey something important, something someone could use in future work with Olga.

The psychologist loses her footing

Supervision session 1

Jenny arrives at the first supervision session full of anticipation. She is troubled and does not know where to start. Our focus will depend on what material Olga gives her psychologist. I wait until I hear what Jenny has to say. My suggestion is that Jenny can start off our sessions by telling me about selected parts of her therapy sessions with Olga. She does not need to try to tell me about everything that takes place, because that is not at all necessary. We will devote ourselves to topics that present obstacles in the therapeutic process. I am going to try to help Jenny identify what these obstacles are.

Through our discussions I want Jenny to regain the competence and creativity that she says she has lost. This is necessary if she is going to help Olga communicate in ways other than statements of just a few words. Jenny has met her patient three times and does not know how to proceed. She is puzzled by the turn the situation has taken and is happy to receive supervision. Olga will be seeing her therapist twelve times, and Jenny and I plan four supervision sessions to be spread throughout that time period.

Jenny tells me how she came to accept Olga as a patient. The mum called again, about six months after Olga had discontinued her therapy with Gudrun. She asked that Olga get to see another psychologist. The school term had just begun, and her daughter was not doing well psychically. Jenny offered to take Olga and give her short-term therapy, once a week, twelve times. Her parents were happy for this opportunity, but not Olga. She had not been part of the decision to switch. They tried to sweet-talk her into going to see Jenny, but in the end they had to use mild force to get her into the car for the first therapy session. Olga accepted this since her protests were usually mild and did not last long. The parents, who were deeply worried about their daughter, at the same time started a series of support sessions with Ingegerd, the psychologist to whom they had previously talked. When she meets Jenny, Olga refuses in a passive way to do those "childish things that she had done before". She is referring to the things she did with Gudrun.

Olga has delicate features, grey-green eyes and summer-blonde hair pulled together in a messy pony tail the way many young girls wear their hair. She is wearing pink glasses that look good on her. She continues to show, even though she does not always say it, that she prefers her "number one" psychologist over her "number two". She does not want to play, paint, draw, play games or play with the dollhouse. No, nothing. She does not take any initiatives and looks at Jenny with an empty gaze. Each of them sits in an armchair while they talk, or rather, while Jenny asks questions to which Olga gives answers politely but laconically. When asked about how she is doing, Olga answers after a deep sigh, "Fine". Otherwise she answers "don't know" or "haven't thought about it" when Jenny wonders what she is good at or what she likes to do.

Jenny is unable to maintain or follow up on any theme during the sessions. Olga neither denies nor acknowledges any problems. They seem stuck in superficial small talk about this and that. In Jenny's mind she has asked all the questions she can think of, and she is well aware that psychotherapy should be something other than simple questions and ditto answers. Olga has also carefully pointed out that they have already spoken about things whenever Jenny addresses them for the second time or more.

Jenny is frustrated that she has nothing to offer but previously answered questions. She remembers Gudrun's notes in the journal about Olga's separation difficulties and harsh background as well as her low self-esteem. Therefore, she knows that Olga is feeling bad behind her seemingly neutral facade. Jenny is unable to help Olga since she is unable to introduce either depth or breadth to the discussions. Social small talk is not what Olga needs in order to work through her problems. Jenny says she feels like she has lost her professional ability even though she knows that she still has it.

Jenny starts regretting that she has been so quick to accept a patient who has gone to Gudrun of all people, a psychologist who had seen so many adopted children over so many years. Jenny says that the best-case scenario obviously would have been that everything had worked out and Olga could have continued her therapy with Gudrun. Jenny concludes by saying that she feels shallow and incompetent, yes, almost dumb. She is dissatisfied with herself and the situation. In the midst of everything else, the psychologist who sits so sadly across from me feels so immeasurably sorry for her little patient.

Focus in supervision

I find Jenny courageous for telling me so openly that she has not been able to reach her patient and that she wants help in turning the situation around. Her self-esteem is good and she knows what she can normally handle, even though at the moment, just like Olga, she is emphasizing everything that she cannot handle. She has never previously felt like such a failure in an encounter with a child, which I understand, since Jenny radiates both competence and warm empathy in a way that children usually like.

As a supervisor for psychotherapists I do not meet their patients but from the vivid description I receive I see a girl in front of me who has a hard time trusting both herself and others. These problems become particularly obvious when it comes to meeting new people or doing schoolwork or other activities that call for some skill. Spontaneously, she cannot say a single thing that is good about herself. She shares her difficulties in saying goodbye to people and her low self-esteem with many other adopted children with heavy baggage.

During our supervision sessions I want to help Jenny find other angles of approach so that she can reach Olga in a way that encourages some mutual give and take. As it stands now, the child, through her quietly dismissive behaviour, is making it difficult for the psychologist to do her job. From experience I know it is possible to land, involuntarily, in such a strong psychological force field with a child that you feel psychologically hand-tied. For a time, you lose your ability to help. Something like that seems to have happened to Jenny. I am going to focus on the necessity of breaking this state within Jenny so that she can yet again become realistic in regard to her view of her own competence. Only when this happens can she help Olga achieve a more realistic view of herself and of her capabilities.

Jenny says in her eagerness that she, too, wants us to focus on what she is doing that is wrong. I agree, but only to a point. It is also important that we analyze those positive things that Jenny is doing to move the psychological process forward. I want balance in our supervision sessions, the balance which is now lacking in the therapy sessions. The intention when it comes to supervision sessions as well as therapy sessions is to have a balanced content, with both pluses and minuses. My overarching goal as a supervisor is to help psychologists realize their strong and weak sides in their meetings with children who have problems like those of Olga. It is often a hard struggle to build a deeper relationship with children who see everything they do as a failure. But it is also all the more satisfying when that relationship begins to evolve and thrive. I want Jenny to experience the feeling of gradually reaching Olga.

Focus in therapy

After having talked about the focus for the supervision, we move on to the focus for Olga's therapy. Since she and Jenny have arrived at something that can be likened to a psychological dead end, I suggest a fresh start where Jenny should clarify for Olga why she is in therapy. She might have forgotten. Jenny needs to describe what Olga's parents told her when they signed Olga up for therapy. Olga needs to know what Jenny knows about the circumstances. Maybe she knew at one point but has forgotten this as well since it was such a long time ago. Olga also has not been sufficiently prepared, and even less motivated, to start with a new psychologist. I further sense that the child does not know what is expected of her now when she thinks it is childish to play games. And it is true that a ten-and-a-half-year-old does not have to enjoy playing with toys any longer. Olga should get a chance to hear this.

From what Jenny tells me about her feelings, I understand that she has gradually felt more and more uncomfortable in Olga's presence. She therefore has filled the silence with a volley of questions, as is easily done when you are stressed. We talk about how Jenny has to pull back a little and wait for Olga. But she still has to show a clear interest in the child and in that way get Olga interested in Jenny and in the ideas that she can come up with. Olga has a psychological space of her own within the therapy, and Jenny must get her to use it. It will probably be easier for Olga once she gets the chance to hear the reasons behind and the goal of her therapy again.

Jenny should start by repeating the number of times they will be meeting. This is particularly important for children who have experienced dramatic separations, which she, being adopted, has. Olga has a hard time with goodbyes, and before she can start benefiting from the therapy, she has to be aware of its duration and its exact ending date. Jenny says she will make a calendar with all of the meeting dates entered on it. At the end of each session Olga will get to cross out the day's date. There are nine more dates, making twelve altogether, which is what Jenny and the parents have agreed on.

My belief is that Jenny, with a different approach, will be able to influence Olga to dare both to give and to accept contact. After that is achieved they can focus on Olga's feelings of inadequacy and, just as important, highlight her capabilities. She seems so insecure about her abilities compared to those of her peers. The problem is, says Jenny, that Olga does not give her anything to work with, since she does not want to talk or play. But I do not see it that way. On the contrary, her refusal to work or play or even talk much is exactly her way of giving Jenny something. She clearly conveys a feeling of inner emptiness, and in this emptiness there is a lot for a child psychologist to work with.

Jenny says she really wants to try to help Olga work through the feelings she has about being abandoned and worthless. If a friend walks away from her, Olga thinks it is because the friend does not find her interesting enough to spend time with. With better self-esteem she will dare to seek out new friends. Jenny wants to try to create a climate during their sessions in which Olga dares to approach her various feelings of inadequacy. I see it the same way. This is exactly what Jenny must do. Together with Olga she needs to put words to Olga's feelings and show her there is nothing strange about them. Jenny's body language and choice of words are important here. She must avoid a tone of voice that conveys any of her own feelings of inadequacy. She also must not indirectly sympathize about how sad it is that Gudrun, the other psychologist, has quit.

We talk about how Jenny now must emphasize that she is the one who will help Olga. Jenny has to be careful not to show she is hurt if Olga happens to say once again that Gudrun was better. This does not need to mean that she does not like Jenny. It is rather a way for Olga to show her deeply rooted fear of break-ups and changes. But letting Olga continue to assert that her first psychologist was better than Jenny is not constructive. It prevents her from accepting help from another psychologist. I emphasize that Jenny must not compare herself to Gudrun. She has to use the knowledge she has received from Gudrun, since she has listened to Gudrun's lectures, but transform this knowledge so that it fits her and this specific patient. In this way I am sure that Jenny will find her own psychotherapeutic style and feel comfortable with it.

Jenny wishes that Olga, aside from talking about things that weigh her down in everyday life, would be able to talk about her background history. Here, though, I do not completely agree with Jenny's ambitions. It is sufficient if Olga can approach *certain* parts of her background. And this will only work if she feels free to choose. We obviously have to be hopeful about what can be achieved through therapy, but it is also important to be realistic in our optimism. As I see it, first and foremost, Olga needs help in managing her day-to-day life, at home and particularly with school friends. To have close friends during the school years can constitute the crucial difference between a happy and an unhappy childhood.

For Olga it is important to build up her self-esteem so she dares to see herself as a likeable friend. If she wants to find out more about her background, she can do that when she gets older and has a more stable psychic ground to stand on.

I suspect that many people in Olga's presence feel just as inadequate as Jenny does. I recognize this phenomenon from meetings with children who have had a deficient start in life and feel second-rate. In order not to be "contaminated" by such a child's feelings of inferiority, the therapist has to find and accentuate the communication that works. Communication that thrives on that second-rate feeling must be disarmed or avoided.

It is the psychologist who has to help the child find navigable pathways. Olga no longer wants to do childish things. She is indeed six months older than when she saw Gudrun and engaged in childish play, but Olga's attitude probably also indicates that she is on guard about delving into the past. Childish things belong in early childhood, and that is when Olga, among other things, was bitten by a rat. Presently, it is too horrifying for her to approach things that happened a long time ago as well as some time ago.

Jenny feels so sorry for Olga, who had to live under such deplorable conditions from the time she was only a little baby. I obviously agree that no child should have to experience what Olga probably experienced. But Olga has nothing to gain from awakening this "poor-little-child feeling" in her psychologist. Since Olga arrived in Sweden, I can imagine that people have often viewed her as a poor little child and thereby have not had high enough expectations of her. Such a scenario might have contributed to Olga's knowing so little about herself as a person. Olga needs warm empathy, which I am sure she gets from Jenny, but she also needs to experience expectations that say, "Come on, of course you can do that, of course you know that." An important task for Jenny is to get Olga to want to delve more deeply into herself as a person and learn more about her capabilities. We have observed that Olga is good at showing what she cannot do, but not good at showing what she can do.

It suddenly strikes me that everyone involved has *regrets* in one way or another. When Olga has had a hard time, she has said that she *regrets* being adopted. When her mum has felt inadequate, it has felt as though she *regretted* the adoption. Jenny has also said that she has *regretted* accepting Olga as a patient. Here it is important for me as a supervisor to put my foot down and make sure that Jenny's, and later Olga's, feelings of regret and anxiety find other forms of expression. Ingegerd, who sees Olga's mum and dad as benevolent and kind-hearted people, assures them that they are good enough parents and that they do *not* have anything to *regret* from that standpoint.

When the session is over, Jenny says she feels inspired to "sort out her thoughts" based on what we have talked about. She now wants to try to infuse her insights in a concrete manner into Olga's therapy, so that Olga can indirectly partake of them. That is exactly what supervision in psychotherapy is all about. It will also be stimulating for me to follow Jenny a bit on her way in her work with Olga.

Projective identification: how does it feel?

Supervision session 2

Olga has come to two therapy sessions after Jenny's and my last meeting. In other words, she has been to five sessions in total. Jenny says that when Olga comes up the steps to the therapy room she shows how weak she feels by collapsing on the top steps. She lies down on the steps and says she does not have enough energy to walk up all the "stupid steps". She waves her arms toward Jenny and screams "help". Jenny does not know exactly what she should do, but she tries to avoid pulling Olga up the rest of the steps. Jenny feels embarrassed by the fact that her colleagues hear and see the situation that arises before Olga hauls herself up and comes into the room.

We talk about how Jenny can try to approach the situation when it happens again, which it probably will. I suggest that if Olga lies on the steps and shouts "help", Jenny focus on the meaning behind Olga's call for help instead of on the fact that Olga is lying down. Jenny can stand on the landing above the steps and extend her arms in a welcoming way toward Olga. She can point out all the steps that Olga has had the energy to climb instead of the two that remain. It is likewise important to emphasize that Olga needs to come into the room so that Jenny can give her the help she is calling for.

When Olga finally comes into the room, she looks around and then sits down in an armchair. She wiggles her legs a little and fiddles with some small items she has in her pocket. Jenny wonders why Olga says so little once she has crossed the threshold into the therapy room. Jenny does what she can to create a calm and comfortable atmosphere in the room. But she is not sure that she is getting this across to Olga. I try to calm Jenny and get her to wait patiently, which she does eventually. She holds off a while to let Olga take the initiative, and Olga does. She starts by curiously fingering some games she has not previously seen.

When Jenny draws a schedule with dates and times for their meetings, Olga initially takes part in the activity. But when the dates for their last few meetings approach, Olga is no longer interested. Her face is expressionless. She neither looks happy nor sad, nothing at all. It is strange, Jenny thinks, that a child can become so stone-like in her face. This spreads an aura of uncertainty in the therapy room, and Jenny takes it as criticism toward her. She looks a little embarrassed when she says it, and I notice that she is affected by feeling criticized. She continues to say that at the end of that particular workday, she took a wrong turn on her way home, a behaviour she finds deeply bewildering. She has never before driven the wrong way when going home. She has lived in the same city her whole life. Jenny returns to the fact that she feels lacking in knowledge, mentally sluggish and uncreative in the presence of Olga. Her job as a child psychologist is perhaps too hard for her, she says so quietly that I can barely hear her. That is not my impression at all.

Before Jenny continues, I want us to stop a moment and talk about what is going on in the relationship between Jenny and her patient. There must not be an alliance between Jenny and her patient where they both feel like they do not know anything and cannot do anything. Jenny visualizes this scenario and chuckles. I already suspected at our first meeting that many people who try to help Olga feel incompetent. These thoughts are strengthened now, and I say that Olga is transferring her thoughts of being second-rate to all her "helpers", even Jenny. Since Olga's feelings are so intense, it is easy to identify with them. When Jenny does this she feels as incompetent as Olga does.

Jenny's feelings tell us a lot about the strength of Olga's feelings of inferiority. In this way, she gets Jenny to feel inside how Olga feels inside. This is the girl's way of communicating how she really feels, even though she says with words that she feels fine. But in order to interpret this pattern, the receiver, Jenny, needs to understand what is going on. I therefore want to lay out these psychological mechanisms for Jenny.

Children who see themselves as second-rate, of course, expect second-rate help from second-rate helpers. How could they expect anything else? Judging from Olga's way of relating to others and to life, we fear that what she received early in life was second-rate care and that has contributed to forming her self-image. Without understanding it herself she conveys in therapy her own feelings by making Jenny feel inadequate, dumb and slow. Olga is familiar with these feelings and therefore stages them unconsciously in her encounters with other people. In therapy, however, this has to end immediately. Jenny has to assert her share of the responsibility so that she stops letting Olga "contaminate her with the feeling of being bad at everything".

What Jenny has to offer is not second-rate. Olga also is no second-rate girl. I encourage Jenny to show her patient through a changed approach that she believes in her strength and ability. Jenny must therefore try to feel like a knowledgeable psychologist who gives help of prime quality because Olga is worth it. She has to radiate that she knows a lot about children and that she knows many who are adopted. Jenny must relate to Olga based on what she is *truly* conveying, not based on her laconic behaviour, which gives a confusing message and is leading Jenny down the wrong path.

When I ask Jenny her thoughts about everything I have said, she replies that she feels turned inside out. She realizes that it is anything but desirable for Olga and herself to join together as two lost souls, but she hastens to add that she does not usually feel so "lost". When Jenny understands more about these mechanisms, she will be able to discern her little patient's feelings much faster by trusting and interpreting her own feelings. As a child psychologist she is going to encounter many children who relate to people in the same way as Olga does. When Jenny becomes fully aware of what a psychological force field she is in, she will once again have full access to her own knowledge.

Jenny wonders here about the risk of blaming the child if the communication does not turn out well. I explain that I do not mean that we should always treat a child's questioning of the therapy situation and the therapist as unwarranted. We talk at length about the necessity of training oneself to distinguish between various types of feelings of inadequacy. Negative reactions expressed by children toward child psychologists can certainly be warranted. We certainly do not always know best. Exaggerated refusal to accept outer circumstances, though, can be part of the way a child relates to others and thus be part of her problematic behaviour. A psychologist must be extremely observant and realize that she cannot help a child if she always thinks that feelings of inadequacy are synonymous with her own incompetence. She would be doing the child a disservice by not being alert to this psychological phenomenon.

Olga does not know her own capabilities. However, Jenny, who normally gives both a knowledgeable and a trustworthy impression, can also lose her sense of competence if she takes on Olga's feelings without understanding the psychological connections. Jenny listens and says that during her psychologist training she read about the phenomena referred to as "projective identification" and "parallel psychological processes". She wonders if what she is experiencing might just be a prime example of these phenomena. And here she is exactly right about what is going on! Olga transfers, or projects, her feelings onto Jenny, who takes them into herself and identifies with them. Thereby, Jenny experiences these feelings as her own.

The phenomenon "projective identification" only arises, though, if Jenny first "accepts" and then identifies with the feelings that Olga projects onto her. It is common that people in such situations react the way Jenny does. They do not recognize themselves. For Jenny this meant that after an exhausting therapy session she got lost on her way home, even though it is really Olga who is not finding the right paths to choose now and in the near future. When several people in Olga's immediate circle react with similar feelings of inadequacy, parallel processes come into being.

The adoptive parents, through their talks with Ingegerd, are strengthened in their belief that they are good parents. They are not at all as inferior as they have perceived themselves to be. With sorrow in her voice the mum had said that Olga probably would have fared better as a foster child with the Russian woman at the orphanage. We get back to the topic of regret again. Jenny, too, as we remember, has thought it would have been better for Olga to have continued her therapy with Gudrun, even though she knows that it did not work out that way. And Olga has shocked her parents by saying that she regrets being adopted. She does not know what this implies, but the statement has frightened and saddened her parents. All these parallel processes of regret must be broken! This is absolutely essential if Olga is to have a chance of being a prime choice as a daughter, as a patient and as a friend!

Jenny thinks it is astounding that she could have been so strongly pulled into such a force field without noticing it herself. But this is not unusual in psychotherapeutic work. The supervisor's task is to help trace the origin of the resulting feelings because it is only then that the contamination can be stopped. Then Jenny continues by describing her latest session with Olga. She says that Olga became more and more talkative toward the end of that session. She had tried to count the steps up to the therapy room, but tells Jenny that she lost count after some point. But the staircases at the Erica Foundation are long, and it takes many steps to climb them. Olga says that her mum's birthday is coming up soon, but she cannot remember when. She mumbles something about a present she has made. She pulls her books out of her satchel and shows them to Jenny. She says that she has homework in reading and math but that she is not good at math. She also mentions that she has been at an indoor public pool with her dad but that she can only swim, not dive.

Easy to show what she cannot do – hard to show what she can do

Jenny listens first and then says that Olga is good at showing what she cannot do but not so good at showing what she can do. Jenny wants to help her change that. She mentions as examples that Olga has just told her that she can count a fair number of steps on the staircase, she has made a present for her mum's birthday, she can swim and she can manage her reading assignment. Jenny waits quietly for the words to sink in with Olga, who looks confused. She recognizes her own words in what Jenny has said, but they sound the opposite. Jenny says she cannot help smiling while Olga tries to figure out how the sentences became so strange.

Jenny is persistent and wants to talk more about what Olga can do and does know. She wants to tell Olga what these things are since Olga cannot come up with them on her own. I praise Jenny here for her ability to find an entry into the theme with Olga of can/cannot so quickly. She has reproduced Olga's own words without changing the content, but she has emphasized Olga's capabilities instead of her shortcomings. Jenny is closing the gap with Olga, who is starting to sense that something good can come out of her therapy. Jenny rounds off by saying that all children benefit from knowing what they are capable of. Olga answers with a smile at the thought that there might actually be things that are good about her.

During the sessions the schedule is out in plain sight, and Olga gets to cross out the day's date after each session. With this Jenny wants to show that if you plan to bid farewell it becomes less painful. She repeats that they are going to meet a total of twelve times, neither more nor fewer. The twelfth hour is the last one and at that point they will shake hands and say goodbye. Olga needs to hear this to lessen the anxiety that is awakened in her at the mere thought of having to say goodbye. Her reaction is not unusual for an adopted child, who has experienced the profoundest of all goodbyes. The fear of being abandoned is so close at hand that it is quickly activated. This happens even though Olga has a loving family. It takes time for children to build up the capability for feeling trust in other people, if they have not received enough help with attachment in the early stages of life.

Olga still insists that she does not want to engage in childish things in therapy. Jenny and I speak about the importance of relating respectfully toward children when you suspect that they are signalling fear in the face of being reminded of difficult circumstances. Jenny further points out that she has received the results of the aptitude test that Olga has taken. Olga's parents have asked Jenny to go through the results with their daughter. They also think it would be good for Olga to understand more about how much she knows. The rest of the supervision time today is devoted to planning how Jenny best can convey this to Olga. It is important that there is a dialogue between them when they go through the results of the various parts of the test. Jenny can start by reminding Olga that the test shows what children are capable of. Then she can go over to saying that she now wants to tell Olga what she has managed.

Individual presentations of test results should always start with the parts of the test with the best results and then proceed to those with less good results. With this in mind Jenny must try to get Olga to understand what types of tasks she manages well versus those she manages less well and therefore must practice more on. Jenny, with her knowledge of what is appropriate and necessary to know at the age of ten, needs to guide Olga toward this understanding. There is, however, a lot that a child of ten does not yet need to know. My experience tells me that children who are insecure about their capabilities are also unaware of their peers' capabilities and therefore need to hear examples of such.

Jenny sighs and says with a slight smile that there is so much to think about when working with children in psychotherapy. I can only agree, but the more practice, the more skill. She concludes the hour by saying that she wants to try to find out the meaning of the Russian words that Gudrun had jotted down. Maybe they can contain some kind of message?

Nettle whip

Supervision session 3

Olga has been to seven therapy sessions when Jenny and I meet for the third time. Jenny is so upset that she can hardly breathe and her face is beet red. Before she has had time to sit down, she starts telling me about the translation of one of the Russian words. It is too horrible. Jenny does not really even want to utter the word, but says it anyway while she is sobbing. It means stinging nettle whip! I also have to catch my breath when I hear this, and I share Jenny's distress. We look at each other, and it takes a little time before the full meaning sinks in. The associations we make are to nothing other than pure sadism. It is beyond our comprehension that something like that can be used for child-rearing purposes. We both need to talk about this with each other before we can manage to continue. We do not know what Olga has experienced, but the mere fact that she knows such a word is terrible enough. It strengthens the impression that she has had an extremely harsh early childhood.

Jenny has received this information second-hand. I emphasize that as a child psychologist you have to deal extremely cautiously with information that you do not receive directly from children or parents. This is nothing that Olga has expressed outright. She has only mumbled it to herself or possibly to Gudrun. Despite everything, it is important for Jenny to stick to the themes that we have agreed should be the focus for the therapy and not steer the dialogue toward what this terrible thing might mean. Olga is only seeing Jenny five more times, and I do not judge this as the right time for Olga to approach overwhelmingly difficult things from her early childhood. She is only ten years old, and she needs all her energy just to manage day-to-day life with school and friends. More than anything else she needs to become psychically stronger before she can start working through her background.

Jenny goes over to telling me that it is becoming easier and easier for Olga to step into the therapy room. Now that Jenny shows that she believes in Olga's ability to take care of things herself, Olga no longer loses her energy at the top steps. The atmosphere during the sessions also feels lighter. Jenny has talked to Olga about the fact that it is difficult to change psychologists. Olga answers bluntly that she would rather have gone to Gudrun "who was good at understanding". Jenny is happy that Olga uses the past tense and gladly acknowledges Gudrun's skill. Jenny tells Olga that she herself has also learned a lot from Gudrun, who has been her teacher. That is why she also knows so much about how to help children. Olga gets a curious look in her eyes when she hears this. Here I give Jenny praise for her excellent way of handling Olga's bluntness, not taking it as criticism but rather doing something constructive with it. Well done. They realize that they both have a link to Gudrun, and after this, Olga does not need to ask for her any more.

When Olga glances at the chart with dates for all the therapy sessions, Jenny takes the opportunity to emphasize how many times they have met and how many times they will meet before concluding. It is important for Olga to hear how much time she actually will get so that they do not only concentrate on the time that she will not get. Jenny, who now better understands Olga's fear of unprepared endings, therefore repeats the date for their last session. She adds that the two of them have agreed on how many times they are going to meet and that this is not going to change. Olga wants to hear about the agreement over and over again. It seems to make her feel secure while at the same time she protests in her quiet way and says that she herself has not actually agreed on anything.

Here in fact I have to agree with Olga, which I point out to Jenny. She has in all likelihood never agreed with anyone about anything important. She can therefore not understand the concept of mutuality. She was taken to the orphanage. Her adoptive parents took her away from the orphanage and brought her to Sweden. Then they took her to Gudrun and afterwards to Jenny, even though she did not really want to see Jenny, just to give a few examples. That is the way her life has looked. I encourage Jenny to deepen Olga's understanding of "mutual agreement" through a few different examples. If Olga is going to make new friends, she has to understand that both parties' words are equally important when an agreement is made.

Aptitude test

Jenny devotes an entire therapy session to the results of the aptitude test that Olga has taken in school. Jenny explains that Olga is going to hear about how she did. She did hear her results at school but that was a while back. Olga does not say no, and Jenny interprets this as indicating that she wants to hear the results. The test consists of two parts. In the one part the child's language ability is tested. Here the pupils get to answer questions on the meaning of words, show how many words they know and show that they understand cause and effect. In the other part they do not need to answer with words. Here they get to show what they know in different ways, through recognizing patterns, doing puzzles or pointing out pieces that are missing in pictures. Sometimes they are put under time-pressure and sometimes they are not. Olga seems to remember the tasks but not how she managed to answer or solve them. She says she liked it best when she did not have to rush, because then it was not so stressful.

Compared to her peers, Olga has average results. What is striking, though, is that she performs somewhat unevenly. When it comes to the *non-verbal* part she receives average results. In the tasks that contain patterns and puzzles or where she is asked to discern differences, she is skilled and fast. Here she can work fast when she is reminded that she is supposed to do so. In the *verbal* part she gets lower scores on the test sections that measure the ability to understand cause and effect. Her vocabulary is more limited than that of her peers. The math problems she manages almost as well as her peers. Considering that Olga missed out on both stimulation and training in her earliest years and also switched mother tongues at the age of five, the results indicate that she actually has a good potential for schoolwork.

After each partial result they have gone through, Jenny asks if Olga has thought about whether she has managed the tasks very well, fairly well or not so well. Olga has no clue. She is completely sincere when she says that she has not thought about it. Jenny wants Olga to start thinking now about what she is good at, what she is fairly good at and what she needs to practice more on in order to know as much as her classmates. I see it as progress that Olga dares to take on this challenging thought. Jenny also continues persistently with converting the test results into examples from everyday life. After a while Olga adds her own ideas. She says that if you are good at math you know how much money you have saved. It is also easier to go shopping by yourself then. Good for you, Olga! She continues and says that if she learns more words, it will be easier to read horse books. Now dad or mum reads out loud to her every evening.

When this session is over, Olga is dazed with tiredness. She yawns, rubs her eyes with her knuckles and leans against the banister as she slowly shuffles down the steps. At the next session, Jenny says, Olga is chattier. They continue to talk about the preceding hour and Jenny wants to repeat some of the test results. She wants to talk more about those things that are positive about Olga. Jenny perseveres even when Olga seems not to be listening. It is not easy for Olga to accept appreciation. She does not know how to do it. Jenny talks to her about how accepting praise is something she has to practice a lot. Olga looks happy. It turns out that Olga remembers almost all the abilities of hers that Jenny pointed out during the previous session. After all this, Olga wants to draw, which she does well.

Using a pencil Olga draws a girl who, she says, is out travelling. The trips, though, seem to be lacking content and are without both a start and a destination. Jenny suggests that they create a make-believe story about the girl and fantasize about where she comes from and where she is going. Olga tries to come up with different ideas about where the girl's trip started. It gets easier when she notices Jenny's confidence in her creative abilities. They talk a little about various destinations for the girl's trip. Jenny and I agree that Olga certainly can give form to her own history when she is free to choose her own method of expression. To transfer her own experiences to the fantasy girl is Olga's way of conveying experiences from her own life's journey. It started in one place whose name she has forgotten and has a destination she has not yet decided.

Jenny asks what the top three wishes of the girl in the drawing are. The answer: "A house, a car and make-up stuff, and when she grows up she wants to take care of horses." After that Jenny asks about Olga's own wishes now and for the future. She says she wants the same things as the girl on the paper. Here Jenny says to Olga that her mum and dad have told Ingegerd that the family has a house and a car, so Olga already has those items. Jenny explains that the house and the car are usually seen as belonging to the whole family. Olga looks puzzled. She has never thought about it that way before. Jenny also shows in a fine way, I think, that she takes Olga's dreams of the future seriously. She says convincingly that she is sure Olga will become a skilled stable groom who can buy nice make-up when she grows up. Jenny also gives confirmation to Olga's wish to increase her vocabulary so she can read her horse books more easily. Olga understands that she has to read many such books to learn more about ponies and other horses. Jenny does what she can to inspire Olga with hope about a good life, both now as a ten-year-old girl and in the future as a grown woman.

Russia: object of fantasies

Olga's parents have told Ingegerd that she has started watching a TV programme about adopted people who are seeking their biological roots. Jenny directs the conversation toward TV programmes in general to see if Olga wants to mention something about "her" programme. She does. She says that it is about people who travel to the country where they were born to see if they like how it looks there. Ingegerd has heard from the parents that Olga in the beginning thought the programme was terrible because you did not know how things would turn out. She watches the programme together with her dad, who assures her that everyone on the show will get to meet a relative. My interpretation is that Olga is clearly conveying how she is capable of approaching her roots. She takes part in other adopted youths' personal histories when the outcome is certain and when she is sitting securely and comfortably next to her dad. Both the parents and Olga know that Ingegerd and Jenny speak to each other occasionally.

A clear change has occurred in Jenny's approach as a psychotherapist. She can switch more freely between maintaining an overall theme on the one hand and taking up what Olga is thinking and doing here and now on the other. I comment that when the psychologist radiates confidence, it usually rubs off on the patient. Jenny, who, as opposed to Olga, can appreciate praise, laughs. As she gradually gets her self-confidence back and thereby appears as the first-rate psychologist that she is, Olga's confidence in her grows. It is no longer incompetence that is the dominating feeling during the sessions. Jenny's persistent walk-through of the test results has meant a lot to Olga, the parents tell Ingegerd. The therapy has meant the start of a more positive self-image for their daughter. Olga laughs now when Jenny raps on the table with her knuckles to underscore that of course Olga can become very good at daring to want to show, both herself and others, things that are good about her.

Toward the end of today's supervision, I remind Jenny that next time we need to talk about the conclusion of Olga's therapy. Before we go our separate ways we mention the terrible stinging nettle whip again. How diabolical! There are no words for what we feel. As a psychologist you sometimes hear things you cannot bear, says Jenny. I agree and that is why you have to have the possibility of getting supervision.

Supervision session 4

After Olga has had ten therapy sessions, Jenny and I meet for the fourth and last time. Jenny thinks things are significantly easier with Olga now. She has become more open in her communication with Jenny, who now looks forward with curiosity to Olga's weekly visit. It turns out that when Olga feels free to approach the topic of her background in her own way and at her own pace, she takes up completely different aspects from what Jenny had anticipated. At one point they sit and talk about different countries, something that often interests adopted children.

Olga says the names of countries that are close to Russia: Belarus and Estonia and some others. They stop to talk about these countries, and after a while Jenny also mentions Russia. Olga quickly says that she does not know where Russia is located. She says it with such conviction that Jenny believes her. She says to me that she took it for granted that Olga would want to see a map of the country where she was born. They "agree" that at the next session they will look at a map.

Jenny forgets at this particular point in time that Olga's parents have told the children a lot about Russia, maybe too much. When Jenny brings an atlas and turns to the page with a map of Russia at the next session, Olga shows no interest whatsoever. She just looks puzzled when Jenny points out Moscow. Olga's surprised expression makes Jenny realize that the two of them never actually "agreed" at all that Olga wanted to look at an atlas. Jenny suggested the map activity with so much conviction that Olga just went along with her without saying anything. Here

I point out, as usually has to be done several times, the importance of keeping the same pace as the patient. The idea about the map is entirely Jenny's and she forgets to "read" Olga to see if she is on board with the agreement.

Jenny wants to convey realistic facts about Russia by using the map, but Olga's thoughts revolve only around the life she lived there and nothing else. I see this as Olga's not having any coherent memories from Russia on her "own inner map". Olga's understanding of her background does not increase through educational explanations of how it is in the real Russia. Her thoughts about that country are purely on the psychological plane. Jenny is too eager here and things are going too fast for Olga, who is not yet ready to devote so much psychic energy to her origins. She answers by going quiet and abruptly stopping the play she is engaged in, the way which children often do when they hear something they are not ready for.

Jenny, realizing she is on the wrong track, withdraws the activity. I admire her for her ability to be flexible when she notices from Olga's response that she is not drawn to any map books. In pure surprise Jenny instead leaves the conversation open to try to catch and follow up on Olga's next signal. The thoughts of Russia, though, have stuck with Olga because suddenly she is brave enough, says Jenny, to ask if a mum can get two children at the same time. Jenny explains that it is possible. Such children are called twins and remain the same age as each other as long as they live. Olga looks puzzled at the answer, which seems too overwhelming for her. Even here Jenny slips into describing in terms of reality what it means to be two children lying together in a mum's stomach. Jenny is being accurate about twins, but Olga is thinking about how she and her brother came about. She is probably also wondering whose stomach is actually involved when it comes to her and her brother.

Olga's background seems complicated and confusing to her. When and where were she and her brother born? And most importantly, by whom? Olga has many unanswered questions, but says with certainty that she and her brother were born at the same time. In one way, I contend, you have to say that the child is right. The siblings psychologically speaking were born on the same day. They were born together a second time when they arrived in Sweden on the same day. Olga's parents did get two children at the same time, although they were not twins. I point out to Jenny that since Olga is only doing short-term therapy, it is enough for her to dare to formulate some of these thoughts. It will make it easier for her to ask the big questions of her mum and dad later on when she is ready for realistic answers.

Now and again Olga has mentioned the names of some classmates, which delights both Jenny and me. This is a sign that she is starting to become interested in new friends. It indicates that her self-image has become stronger and that she dares to believe that another child wants to be with her. When Olga no longer transfers her own feelings of being inadequate to her classmates, they will want to be with her and the vicious cycle will be broken.

Auf Wiedersehen, arrivederci, see you later

What is left for me to discuss with Jenny is the conclusion of therapy. During Olga's last sessions the focus must be on her agony at the thought of having to saying goodbye to each other. They must look forward to a good conclusion in different concrete ways. For example, they need to go through what has happened during the sessions together and talk about how Olga felt at the beginning and how she feels now. When I get ready to take farewell of adopted children in therapy, I usually talk about how taking farewell is an international problem. This concerns both children and adults in all countries. I suggest that Jenny, if Olga is interested, give some examples of this global difficulty. There are so many examples out there of how we try to make farewells less painful. We express ourselves as if we will see each other again even when we know this is not the case. We say, for example, "Auf Wiedersehen, arrivederci, see you later". Olga might feel less alone with her problem if she sees that this difficulty exists no matter where in the world you are from.

There must also be a place in the concluding phase of a therapy to talk about visions and plans for the future, both short-term and long-term, I point out. That a therapy is concluded in a well-thought-out manner is of great importance. A badly planned conclusion evokes feelings of abandonment and can be an obstacle for the patient in seeking help in the future if needed. Hopefully, the well-planned farewell from Jenny can also function as a good precedent for other day-to-day farewells in Olga's life.

We are also approaching Jenny's and my own goodbye. She says that Olga has taught her a lot about how early living conditions affect a child. She is only ten years old, but she has experiences of an entirely different nature from those common to us who were born in Sweden. I feel, as Jenny does, respect and humility toward little survivors like Olga and agree that she has been an extraordinary teacher, having given her diligent student Jenny many new insights. Jenny laughs and says that she is grateful to have had both a teacher and a supervisor.

Jenny thinks she has developed and become less naive and more perceptive through her meetings with Olga and through the supervision she has received. She has become better at "listening in" and "receiving" when children in various ways try to convey difficult experiences. Jenny appreciates my repeatedly pointing out the importance of trying to catch things that children communicate "between the lines" or through symbolic language. Above all, says Jenny, she has learned once and for all how deeply you can be affected to the core of your being by a child's emotional state. She will never forget how crucial it is to understand which feelings belong to which party. She has also understood how important it is for her as the psychologist to radiate competence and empathy. She says that it is actually obvious that patients want to take part of their psychologists' knowledge and are not interested in all of their inabilities. Jenny will call the family in six months for a follow-up talk, and she will let me know how it goes. Jenny and I bid our thanks and farewells.

For me the meetings with Jenny have been stimulating. It has been easy to create a trusting work climate between us, which is just as important in supervision as in a therapy. I have felt free to be frank and convey what I have wanted to Jenny without being worried about offending or hurting her. It is rewarding to supervise people with the traits that Jenny has – enthusiasm and a desire to understand. What she is still lacking is experience, but that usually takes care of itself.

Six months later

After the follow-up conversation with Olga's parents, Jenny calls me to share what has been said. Olga concluded her therapy after a total of twelve sessions, and the farewell phase went well. The effect of the meticulous review of the test results is still there, according to the parents. Olga has an easier time accepting her own good sides. She stands up for herself better and lets people know her boundaries, which has made it easier for her family to communicate with her. She is less sensitive about separation. It is not easy but it goes fairly well if her parents help her prepare for it. She approaches the topic of her adoption now and again with a question to her parents. She has found two new friends in her class, or rather they have found her. Olga is delighted that other children want to have her as a friend. According to the teacher the other children seem surprised that they have not discovered Olga earlier.

Olga is concentrating during lessons and her schoolwork is going more smoothly. She is at school every day and seldom has stomach aches. Every evening she reads a chapter of some horse book that she has borrowed at the school library. Her mum says that Olga has soon read all of the school's books on horses. Her visions of the future remain the same. She wants to be a skilled stable groom and she is now going to start taking riding lessons, which she earlier did not dare to do. It pleases me to hear Jenny talk about how Olga is continuing to plan for the future. That usually means that a child's low spirits are loosing their grip on her. Olga's parents tell Jenny that they also have appreciated their talks with Ingegerd. The talks have made them more confident that they are not inadequate as parents, on the contrary. They feel that they are good enough parents.

Supervision: why?

To meet a child who has had traumatic experiences always brings on feelings of great intensity. It is undeniably demanding but also extraordinarily gratifying when, during a time-limited, short-term therapy, you can succeed in helping children rediscover their joy of life. These children have in different ways suffered personal losses of great magnitude. Both as a professional and as a fellow human being you have intense empathy for the children and their families. In the therapy you share the painful working-through process with the child, but you cannot let yourself be overwhelmed by the past trauma. If you become too deeply affected emotionally by what has happened to the child and identify too closely with him or her, the psychotherapeutic space between the psychologist and the child is lost. It is in this space that the psychologist and the child build up the specific relationship that is necessary for the therapeutic work to take off and to stay in orbit. As a prerequisite for this relationship, the psychologist must be able to let the space remain a psychologically shielded zone where a variety of feelings from the child can come to the fore.

It is mostly when something triggers particularly strong feelings that this ability can falter in the psychologist. What happened to Olga's psychologist Jenny was that she so strongly identified with Olga's feelings that she started experiencing them as her own. She brought both the child's and her own feelings into the therapy without being able to differentiate between them. Jenny realized that she needed supervision when she was not able to create the psychological space where the two of them were meant to interact. There was therefore no therapeutic relationship between them initially. Instead their dialogue continued to consist of small talk without relevance or depth. Jenny needed supervision to be able to give Olga the therapy she so greatly needed but denied that she wanted. In order to create a therapeutic relationship it is necessary for the psychotherapist, aside from being well qualified, to feel secure with her work method.

To be able to maintain a secure and stable approach in particularly anxiety-ridden situations, those who work with psychotherapy, no matter their age or experience, must have access to supervision when it is needed. If psychologists get a chance to work through difficult experiences they encounter in their work, the risk of their feeling burnt out or exhibiting other symptoms of exhaustion is minimized. The most appropriate form for this working through is supervision. By caring about psychologists' psychic well-being, we increase the quality along with the quantity of the therapeutic work.

When I as a psychotherapist take on the role of a supervisor I change my perspective. The supervision session is an educational situation, not a treatment one. The goal of supervision is to help the psychologist integrate theoretical knowledge into his or her practical therapeutic work. In supervision there must be an open atmosphere so that psychologists find it possible to bring up their own shortcomings. This is particularly important since as a therapist you use yourself as a tool for your work. It can no doubt be difficult to take a critical look at yourself when you are unsure of whether you have succeeded well enough in your work. That is how Jenny felt when she called upon me for help.

A common and easily made mistake in psychotherapy with children is that the psychologist becomes too eager, particularly if she is still not so experienced. The pace of the work becomes much too rapid for the child. You can never rush a child's psychic healing, only facilitate it. How to adapt the ebb and flow to the child who is in therapy is often an important theme in supervision. Children must get the time they need in order to develop at their own pace. Accordingly, the supervisor must also adapt the discussion pace to the psychologist's pace. If the pace is too rapid in the supervision session, there is a great risk that the already forced pace in the child's therapy will continue. Children in such situations respond by breaking off their play or by not listening. It is therefore necessary for the supervisor to introduce a tempo with which the psychologist feels comfortable. For both parties it is most often a matter of listening more and talking less.

Therapeutic meetings with children require a constant psychological presence, which leads to many tough situations. The goal for the person who is receiving supervision is to become more skilled in psychically demanding situations, and when she succeeds, she will develop further in her professional role. We can only speculate about what would have happened if Jenny had not received supervision in her work with Olga. A feeling of incompetence and failure probably would have prevailed in Jenny, Olga and Olga's parents. Olga probably would have felt that she had failed as a patient if she had not been able to reap any benefits from her therapy. Jenny might have lost interest in working with children with psychic disturbances from early childhood and sought out a different specialty within the profession. Olga's mum, who had unrealistically high expectations of her daughter's therapist and of herself as a parent, would probably have continued to feel like a failed mum. The feeling of regret might also have remained with each and every one of them.

To be a supervisor for those who work in various people-care professions and who want to develop further in their professional roles is inspiring and mutually enriching. It is not only the person who receives supervision who acquires new knowledge. As a supervisor you constantly get new impulses, which lead to stimulating discussions and which time after time contribute to the rethinking and redeveloping of your own positions.

4 A mother's trauma becomes her son's trauma

Ali, seven years old, undergoes a psychological assessment

Mother and son have an interwoven life history

Ali's mum calls on the advice of Ali's school and asks for help for her son, who is seven years old. He has attended about half of his first year of school. His teacher has urged the mum to seek help for Ali. She says on the phone that her son is disruptive and makes trouble for children as well as adults at the school. The mother, whose name is Aisha, comes for a consultation and tells me about the school's problems with Ali. Aisha is in her mid-thirties, was born and raised in Iraq and has lived in Sweden for the past seven years. She gives a kind impression and is eager for Ali to behave in school. She looks sad and has a tired gaze.

Aisha says that the school situation is untenable for Ali, according to his teacher. He is incapable of accepting help or of being corrected and has problems getting along with his peers. He is rough toward the other children and can go to attack without any reason. He says he is going to kill them. Ali seems on guard for attack and is difficult to reach, gives people the finger in an obscene gesture and hisses "fuck you" to the personnel. He has stopped going to after-school care. It was too much of a strain for him. It was too hectic there with too many children and too few adults. Aisha does not mistrust the teachers but has a hard time believing that her son could have such big problems and behave so badly. She thinks it is possible that he is easily influenced by other children who fight and tease.

When I ask how Aisha sees her son, she describes him as a clever boy who always wants to be independent. He seldom asks for help. At home things go smoothly most of the time, but there are only the two of them. Ali speaks both Arabic and Swedish well. Lately he has started answering his mother in Swedish when she speaks Arabic. She was eager for Ali to learn Swedish and therefore sought out a preschool where the children spoke Swedish even though it meant a long commute. At home Ali likes to play computer games, collect flags and play with robots and dinosaurs. Sometimes he plays war, but Aisha does not like that. She tries to prevent him but is not successful even though she tells him how sad it makes her when he plays war.

When Aisha decided to leave her home country and come to Sweden, she was pregnant with Ali without knowing it. She had completed her studies in nursing and also in surgical nursing. Ali's father is a compatriot who still lives in Iraq. She briefly speaks about the fact that the father could not leave his relatives and move abroad and that Aisha could not conceive of moving back after everything she experienced during the war. It is in Sweden she wants to live with her son. The relationship with Ali's father is neither good nor bad but neutral, says Aisha. I notice that she does not want to talk about Ali's father but concludes by saying that he sends them money every month. Aisha has not been able to bring herself to travel to Iraq even for a short visit since she came to Sweden. She would be overwhelmed by too many painful memories, she explains. Nor does she have any close relatives remaining in Iraq. Both her brothers live in Sweden. Her father died shortly after she left the country, and her mother died several years ago.

Aisha is insistent about not wanting to talk about her departure from her country and the reasons behind it. She says she struggles every day not to think about what happened and that she hopes she can forget. I let her know that she only needs to tell me things she thinks might help me understand her son. I do not need to know more than that. Swedes ask her about the war, "but there is not a single Swede who understands what happens in war", she says. When it comes to me she is absolutely right. But I also explain that even if I cannot comprehend the cruelties of war experiences, I do know a lot about how traumatic experiences affect people and in turn their children. My thought is that this knowledge may be useful for me when I meet Ali. But I do not verbalize this to Aisha.

I ask Aisha what Ali knows about their background, and she says they never talk about it. Ali does not think about the fact that his mother is from Iraq, other than when he comments that she pronounces some Swedish word in a particularly strange way. During the conversation Aisha apologizes for her bad Swedish and looks at me inquiringly to see if I understand what she is saying. It is not difficult at all to understand her. She has a marked accent but her grammar is good. I only have to speak a little more slowly than usual, and Aisha understands everything I say.

When Aisha came to Sweden she was eager to learn Swedish in order to be able to start working. It has been difficult for her to find a permanent job, but she has had various short-term contracts within senior services. She was unemployed for a while but has now taken a course in medical Swedish and has landed a job within her specialty at a hospital in a town about sixty miles from Stockholm. She is really pleased about it and says "finally". She sought out the location because one of her brothers lives there with his wife and three sons. Ali's uncle, Hamid, is devoted to his nephew, and Ali likes spending time with him and his family. In six months she plans for her and Ali to move there, so she has started looking for a flat in close proximity to her relatives.

Since there are such major problems at school, Aisha would like for Ali to get a chance to come and see me a few times. She hopes this might help. I explain that in that case he will undergo a psychological assessment during which I will give him various tasks. He will be asked to draw, paint, answer questions and talk about pictures. He will also get to do other things that children usually like to do, such as building with toys in a sand tray. The assessment will naturally include talks between Ali and me.

I describe the different parts of the assessment thoroughly because I want to make sure that Aisha understands the purpose of Ali's visits with me. A psychological assessment is something completely different from just meeting with a psychologist a few times. By looking at Ali's assessment results, I will try to understand the reasons behind his behaviour and symptoms. When we understand the causal connections, it will be easier for both Aisha and others to help Ali, I tell her. She listens carefully, but she is not used to this kind of reasoning. Aisha looks a little hesitant, so I tell her to think about everything before deciding. She wants to talk to her brother and sister-in-law first. She hopes that Ali does not end up at the back of the queue if she does not say yes right away. It is her brother's Swedish wife who has told her to inquire about this matter of the queue. I assure her that he will retain his place in the queue while she is considering the matter. Aisha calls me after a few days and says yes to the psychological assessment.

The psychological assessment of Ali takes place during four meetings, and I really have to exert myself to the fullest to carry it out. The meetings are sweaty and loud and much more takes place than I can describe here since I will focus on the content that illustrates the probable reasons for Ali's difficulties. I describe what Ali does and how I approach him both when he is cooperating well and when he does not cooperate but instead does his own thing. Gradually, I understand more and more of what he is trying to convey behind his attitude, and I describe that. Finally, I summarize the results from the assessment and share the content of the three talks with Aisha. Ali's uncle Hamid participates in the third of Aisha's sessions.

Ali presents his backside

Session 1

Ali arrives with his mum, and she follows him into my room. He is wearing a black baseball cap with a skull on it. The visor is pulled down over his eyes. He makes it obvious that he is not going to take off the cap. His shoulder-length brown hair is tussled. His body is large and stable, and physically he gives the impression of being older than his seven years. Ali is carrying a plastic bag with toys. Maybe he feels more secure if he has his own stuff with him. He follows me into the room without being able to see much from under the visor. He does not say bye to his mum, who calls "See you soon" several times in a voice pleading for a response before she goes to the waiting room.

Ali stands broad-legged with his back to me in the middle of the room so I introduce myself speaking to his back. He does not answer, and he does not even dignify my feet with a look. He is not trying to peek under his cap, which most children would do after a while out of pure curiosity. I ask him something about his school. He answers in a nonsensical manner, and I am not meant to understand what he is saying. I ask again, and he says in a sassy way:

What d'ya think?

I say:

If you want, you can put your cap on the chair.

Ali answers peevishly:

I'll never wanna.
Oh, so you don't want to?
Yeah, 'cause it's so ugly if I do.

I do not fully understand what it is that is so ugly, but it seems sad that Ali's first way of introducing himself is by showing his backside. From the get-go he conveys that there is something negative about his front side, and therefore he chooses to show me his best side, the back of him. I let him remain standing with his back to me, while I chat about how he should feel free to build in the sand tray. But he does what he can to ignore me and make me feel as if I am not worth the time of day. Maybe Ali is used to treating people this way and then seeing that he can indeed make them feel worthless. In any event, it is an effective way he has of keeping people at a distance.

After a fairly long while Ali starts mimicking Michael Jackson's song and dance style, still turned away from me.

I also liked Michael Jackson. He sang and danced really well, I say, in an effort to find some common ground between us.

No answer from Ali, but Michael was most certainly his idol. He has put lots of practice into the steps because he is skilled at dancing around in the pop icon's manner with his back to me.

But Michael did some strange things too, I try.

There are undeniably different reasons for being impressed with Michael Jackson, his song and dance style, his special moonwalk or his various ways of pushing the limits. Not a peep from Ali. Still silent he starts pulling things out of his plastic bag. He turns to the side so I can see robots and skulls, which he places on the floor.

I've built them, Ali states matter-of-factly.
I see.

He battles with them in a strange way. The robots and the skulls aim not at each other but indiscriminately in all directions. Some of them shoot their own kind in the back of the head, others are aiming for Ali. He does not divide the figures into good and evil or into different teams like most children his age do when they play war. He screeches:

Bang, boom, splash!

The sounds are not synchronized with what is happening in the game. Both the figures who are attacking and those who are attacked get killed. When everyone is dead, the game ends and he puts the toys back into the bag. In the game Ali finds no other way out than chaos and death.

Without my making the slightest gesture toward his robots, he makes it clear that I may not touch them. The figures are so important to him that he carefully ties up the bag so that nothing will fall out. When he has fixed the bag the way he wants it, I suggest that he build with the items in the sand tray. He mocks me and my ridiculous old things for a while, but then he simply must take a look toward the toy cupboard, at the same time being sure to let me see his distaste. I ignore his efforts to provoke me with his attitude.

Games reflect inner chaos

Against his own will Ali is gradually drawn to the sand and the toys. He cannot resist. He places houses and trees in rows across the sand tray in something that looks like a little town. It looks neat and orderly all the way until he throws in canons:

They're gonna bomb all the houses.

He knocks over the entire town and snatches more and more things out of the toy cupboard. He puts a volcano on a couch next to a handful of fallen soldiers. A fire lands under a little dollhouse bed. He puts out, or rather throws out, more and more toys. He still has his visor pulled down over his eyes. When I ask him what is happening, he answers something inaudible with a hostile voice. Ali conveys a feeling of inner chaos in his play. His construction degenerates from portraying a town with streets and trees into becoming just one big violently chaotic scene. He takes a fence in his hand and asks sarcastically:

And what's this crap?

Ali does not wait for my answer but says condescendingly:

All the stuff here's so ugly and babyish.

I do not agree with him:

Even if you don't think all the toys here are great, you can still build with them. They're okay if they're good enough to build with, and they are.

What a wacko thing to say, mumbles Ali as he takes more fence pieces and sets them up in the sand.

It looks like he is trying to fence in the destruction he has caused. But when it does not work he shuffles the whole mess of toys to one edge of the sand tray. In doing so he gets a free spot toward the other edge when he can start over with his construction.

Next Ali sets out a tow truck and an ambulance in the sand. With his back toward me he hums motor noises as he drives around with these two vehicles that are normally meant to help people in distress. A hearse stands still at the edge. He packs the ambulance full of sand, which he calls "shit", so that it cannot pick up anyone who is in need. The tow truck is driving far too fast, rolls over and lands upside down. It can therefore not help anyone either. The hearse is the only vehicle not affected. In most of his games Ali sets a scene of chaotic helplessness. There is no help to be had. The vehicles that are supposed to help people become buried in dirt and rendered out of commission. The only vehicle that makes it to the rescue does so when no one needs help any longer.

After this Ali plays with cowboys, tigers, lions and his own robots, which he roughly throws around. He shouts that he is going to destroy them because they are ugly. The cap is no longer pulled down quite as far on his forehead. He is not inviting contact, but it is actually possible to get a short conversation going. I want the cowboys, the soldiers, the wild animals and the robots to be part of the game, too, even if they in various ways destroy and kill. They, too, have needs that have to be satisfied. I say this because he seems to identify partly with such animals and figures as destroy and kill. He does not see any clear line between victim and perpetrator. He does not know which side to root for or to identify with, the strong or the weak. In his games he does not use any figures other than those who are known for killing.

He goes on building in the sand and suddenly says:

People're inside their houses and they're gonna get killed. Yeah, the ones who're standing there are shooting people. They're not gonna make it.

I wonder:

Who are the ones who aren't going to make it?
No one's gonna make it.
Why are the people going to be shot?
I hate them. I hate Christmas trees. Quiet! Fuck you!

I just let that last remark pass, but I say firmly:

I always talk to children who come to see me. I want to do that. And I want to talk to you too.

Ali pretends that the soldiers are making a phone call, and I ask:

What are they saying?
That they're gonna kill everyone.

Ali wants to leave the session before time is up, which I do not go along with. He screams:

But we're gonna see my aunt after this crap today.

What's her name? I ask to calm the situation down.

She's a zero. Never mind her. I've got an uncle. One and zero can make ten, he hastens to add.

Maybe Uncle Hamid, his mum's brother, is a ten-pointer in Ali's eyes. I want to show him that one person may be top-notch, but that does not automatically mean the other person is worthless. Both can be all right. You can like several people at the same time. I comment out loud:

You can like both your aunt and your uncle. You're obviously looking forward to seeing your aunt today since you're in such a hurry.

Ali looks around the room now that his cap is no longer blocking his vision and starts spouting off all the things he sees that he does not like:

Everything's ugly, the desk, that couch, the lamps that are nailed to the wall and no elevator. Crap, just crap.

Lucky, I think, that he does not list me among those things. That means he does not view me as a worthless thing, but at least sees me as a human.

But it's me you're here to see, you know. You're not here to sit at my desk or ride the elevator up and down. I'm not bad at any rate. I promise you.

No answer from Ali.

I want to tell you once again that my name is Elisabeth so you remember that.

When he hears my name he laughs condescendingly and remarks at lightning speed:

That sounds like an old Christmas tree that's lost all its needles and has broken lights.

I cannot resist laughing. I laugh, amused at his relentless attempts to try to make me feel like a rubbish pile. He becomes somewhat rattled at the situational change that arises when I start laughing. There is something touching about Ali's way of calling to battle. He does not realize that he can be both witty and quick. He pulls his cap down in order not to show his uncertainty. It does not occur to him that he is showing his embarrassment via the expressions I can see around his mouth. Before he can add that the ratty-looking tree has messy glitter and that the star is crooked, I take the opportunity to make my own addition to his narrative:

There are also nice Christmas trees that light up the darkness and that smell good.

Ali loses his footing and does not know how to react. An almost invisible smile comes over his face. Maybe he senses the message I am trying to convey, namely, that there is good quality in what I have to offer him, including the items in the room, my knowledge and myself. So I continue:

I know a lot about how children usually think and feel.

Oh, no you don't. You don't know anything, nothing, zero, says Ali, but sounds somewhat less provoking.

Oh, yes I do. Actually, I do know a whole lot. But not exactly everything; you're right if that's what you mean, I answer, remembering what Aisha has said about Swedes and war.

The hour is coming to an end, and I say that we will go to his mum in the waiting room. In response Ali, without warning, takes out one of his robots and whacks it against my shin. He is quite a marksman. He puts a blank expression on his face as if nothing has happened, but my leg is pounding and it hurts. I get angry and show him by using a stern voice that I do not accept having the limits exceeded like this.

Ouch, ouch. It was wrong of you to do that. My leg hurts, I say and point to my leg.

I take a firm grasp of Ali's arm and hold him tightly to make sure he does not repeat his action. He then starts flapping around and screaming at the top of his lungs so that the sound echoes throughout the entire stairwell outside the room:

She's hitting me! She's hitting me! Please don't hit me!

He screams even more loudly:

Ouch! Ouch! Help! Help!

I say sternly:

Be quiet, Ali! Stop that! Nobody hits children here! And children aren't allowed to hit anyone, either. I make sure of that. You don't need to scream for help. You're coming to see me to get help, you know! I'm here helping you.

I make it clear that under no circumstances do I accept his behaviour. At the same time I convey to him that I understand his situation. It is not easy for him to know how to behave when he comes to see a psychologist at the Erica Foundation. This is only his first session.

I'm going to tell you what usually happens here and how people usually behave. You don't know because you haven't been here before. But I know because I'm here every day.

He appears to be at a total loss after having whacked the robot against my leg, where there is now a large red mark.

Fuck you! he hisses.

Listen, Ali! You know what? Those words are not nice and it's getting tiresome to hear them. I know you can say many good words both in Swedish and Arabic. Your mum has told me that.

I have to repeat, both in words and in actions, the four rules that apply to all children who come to see me:

A child never has horrible things happen to him while he's with me. Never! No child is allowed to hurt himself or me. Children are also not allowed to destroy things in the room. This applies to all children. It applies to you. It's my responsibility and I'm the one who decides.

You don't decide here.

Oh, yes I do. These are my rules. They also have to become yours when you come to see me.

Ali gets ready to start screaming again but I am one step ahead of him and say:

You're going to be completely quiet now and listen to me. I have something important to say.

A pedagogical finesse like speaking really softly and waiting for Ali to quiet down in order to hear me will not work. When he is quiet for a moment, I deliver the important message:

You're going to get a chance to come and see me three more times.

Ali looks completely taken aback but remains quiet. I need to see him four times to understand more about what he is lacking. I hold up four fingers in the air to clarify the number of times. He responds by giving me the finger.

No, Ali, that's only one finger. It must be four! We're going to meet three more times. That makes a total of four.

At this point I say the time is up. He has put his finger in the waistline of his trousers, and I indicate that he needs to go now without further ado. The room is dusty from sand. I understand that it will be a sweaty but exciting challenge to reach Ali. In meeting children with difficulties like Ali's, I have use for everything I have learned in my many years of professional experience. I want him to get a chance to experience a few encounters that are unlike most of the others he has had in the past. I want to communicate with Ali based on what I think he is trying to convey beyond his words and actions. I will not let myself be affected by his negative attitude. I also want to help him show some of his good sides. He is not going to get away with believing he has convinced me that he is a "bad boy".

Such stunts will not work

Session 2

Today I ask Aisha to accompany Ali into the room for just a little bit so I can talk to them both for a moment. Ali is not wearing his baseball cap so I see his whole face for the first time. He has the same shade of brown eyes as his mum and his longish hair is newly washed. Ali stands next to Aisha, who has sat down and we start talking. She says they have started planning their move and have seen a flat that suits them. Ali does not show any emotion when his mum talks about moving and about his forthcoming change of school.

I want to know if they have spoken with each other about why Ali is coming to see me. Aisha answers vaguely that she has told him it is good for children to come and play here if they have problems. Ali's teachers want him to come here and thus Aisha does as well. Ali looks surprised. Based on his mum's vague description, I do not think he understands why he is coming to see me. Therefore, I share with him several reasons why children usually come to see me. I give examples of several problems, among them some of his difficulties. Among other things I say that children come to see me because they have a hard time doing what their teachers tell them to do. I continue by saying that other children have parents who have moved to Sweden from their home countries, even though they might not have wanted to. It is never easy to come to a new country. I feel it is important for both mother and son to hear this. A thought is starting to spire inside me: Do Ali's problems perhaps have something to do with Aisha's earlier experiences, even though I know nothing about what they are?

Ali, who has been standing motionless the whole time, suddenly exclaims:

Never comes from Sweden.

I turn to Aisha to let her answer.

We're going to get Swedish passports and then we're Swedes. Dad and I are from Iraq. You know that, even though you've never been there.

Ali, who is starting to get restless, says:

But the dog's Swedish.

He swings and whacks a stuffed animal, a dog, which he has brought along and says:

I'm gonna throw him down the stairs.

When his mum says that she does not want him to do that, Ali starts hissing and yelling. I do not let this outburst detract me from telling his mum what happened last time:

Last time something happened that absolutely may not happen again and I want you, Aisha, to know about it.

Aisha says:

Yes, good, please tell me. I never get to know anything.
What happened was that Ali threw a robot at my leg and hurt me.

His mum does not understand why something like that happened and asks Ali, but she does not get an answer. I answer in his place:

I believe that you, Ali, don't even have time to think before you do something like that. So you probably don't know why you're doing it either. But it's forbidden to hurt others.

Ali understands what else I am going to tell his mum, so he starts scraping and rattling roughly in the sand tray. It is his attempt to get out of a situation he does not want to be in. But I continue:

The other thing that happened was that when I stopped you, Ali, from hurting me again, you screamed at the top of your lungs that I was hitting you.
Quiet! I decide, screams Ali.

Right now it actually seems as if he believes what he is saying.

It was wrong of you to do that! I state matter-of-factly.

Aisha stares in surprise as I continue to drown out Ali's remarks:

I've spoken to the others who also work here and told them I'm seeing a boy who has screamed that I'm hitting him. And that the boy knows this isn't true.

My intention here is to show Ali that his stunt will not work. In addition, it is disturbing, to say the least, for both me and other visitors when we hear a child screaming that he is getting a beating from his psychologist. I also want to assure Aisha that I would never hit her son, even though Ali might claim such a thing. I do not really trust what Ali might say to his mum about his visits with me, in the unlikely event that he might get the idea to tell her something. I invite Aisha to stay in the room or sit right outside the door if she would feel calmer that way. Aisha seems shocked but not exactly surprised by her son's behaviour and thinks it is best for Ali and me to meet alone.

I say to Ali, who is grumbling about how he should be the one who decides:

Yes, I truly believe that you would like to decide, but now I don't think you know what it is you want. I know what I want. I know what your mum wants. We want you and me to do some tasks together. Say bye to mum now please!

Ali makes a fuss, causes things to rattle around and bumps into his mum, who asks him to stop. But Aisha, who has such a sweet manner, cannot make her voice heard in the hullabaloo. I see that she needs help to get out of the situation. When Ali sees that I am approaching his mum and him, he throws himself on the floor and uses his body to block me. Since I want to help Ali get out of his present state as quickly as possible, I retrieve my voice of authority. Now it is all about using imperatives:

Get up! Right this instant!

I let him know that there are no other options just now. I simply start walking toward him on the floor so that he has to scramble up to get out of my path. I want to help him figure out that there are other ways of behaving than crawling around on the floor and screaming.

Ali whispers, and it sounds like he is talking more to himself than to me:

Fuck you!

I let the words pass, because I do not have so much patience left, and I do not want to let Ali use up the last of it. Aisha looks unhappy and wants to give her son a kiss before she leaves, but he turns around and ducks away from her.

Lots of things unclear

When Ali's mum has left, I take the word:

I want to know what you can do, Ali. That's why you're here to see me. That's why you can't lie on the floor screaming. You know you're a big boy and a clever boy. You're really good at showing what you can't do, but not very skilled at showing what you can do. Maybe it's because you don't know your own abilities. Show me and I'll tell you. It's good for you to know. I'm sure you know what I'm talking about.

After I have marked the limits so emphatically, Ali marches over to the sand tray. His defiance has gone away for the moment. He does not come up with anything to grumble or to be rude about. Calmness settles over the room. After some moments of silence, he fires a glance my way and then does so a second time but now with a hint of interest in a response from me. I want him to know that I am with him, so I give him a nod in response. He starts to build in the sand tray, now that he no longer has to listen to instructions from me. I want to get Ali to dare to test his capabilities. If he does so, he will become familiar with his range of potential from good to bad.

He builds an enclosed world in the middle of the sand tray but all the furniture and the interiors land outside. He makes another enclosed area inside the first one, using the fence pieces that he complained about at his first session. He places wild and tame animals as well as houses, train track booms, aeroplanes and road signs outside these fences. A tree stands on a little dollhouse chair and a monkey sits beside the tree. The beds are made up as though they are waiting for someone. He tries to sort out the animals according to family but does not entirely succeed. Where the wild animals are placed, he has the best house, which is a country estate, as well as petrol stations and a church. Is this perhaps where the best nourishment can be found?

He places two small dollhouse telephones on a table. I prefer to see these as positive symbols to show the potential for communication between two people. His set-up is cram-full but he cannot stop himself. Instead, he fetches more toys. The enclosure materials have disappeared in the muddle. Ali takes out some soldiers and they kill people who are inside their houses. Children who feel secure do not usually make a game where warriors kill dolls that are inside their homes unaware of the evil that is about to befall them. But then Ali does not give the impression of being a child who feels secure.

After a few minutes Ali picks up a motley-coloured cow, holds it in his hand and declares:

This looks like Granddad's cow, my mum's dad's cow. He has cows like this.

I think about how Aisha has said that they do not have any relatives left in Iraq. I wonder about Granddad and his animals:

Do you know any cows?
Granddad has cows but he's dead. He sold 'em when he died. He couldn't take 'em with him into heaven.

I ask:

What was your granddad's name?

Ali states matter-of-factly:

I always forget his name. Dad was dead before I was born. My dad had a farm.
Your dad? I say wonderingly.
Yeah, my dad. But I always forget his name too. I also had some brothers and sisters in Iraq, he says.
Oh really?
Yeah, loads, I know.

This is most probably Ali's way of expressing that he does not know, but really would like to know, the truth about his relatives, and, by virtue of that, about his own history. That his dad lives far away in Iraq and not in Sweden becomes synonymous in his game with his dad perhaps being dead. When I ask Ali what he has built in the sand tray, he answers as though all the animals lived inside the inner enclosure even though they have been placed outside it. Things get confusing. He has a hard time telling me about the scene. He distorts his voice and says:

There aren't any cows in Africa, don't you know that, or are you stupid or something?

Ali puts a cobra in position as if to show me which animals belong in Africa. He ends the session by taking out a crocodile with its jaws open and then playing with the soldiers who are going out to kill. He tests me to see whether he can scare me with the crocodile. He waves it around at me. My position now is the same as it has been earlier. All animals, both wild and tame, as well as warriors, should be allowed in the game. I suggest that I can put the crocodile in a safe place until we meet next time. Ali does not object. He does not want me to go with him to meet his mum in the waiting room. He wants to go on his own, even though he is not sure which doors he needs to open. It is not easy to get Ali to let me extend a helping hand to him. On the way down to the waiting room he pauses on the stairs and pokes a piece of plaster out of a loose place in the wall.

Ali shows in many ways that much is unclear to him when it comes to his family relationships, his mother's origins and his own background.

Both nasty and nice ones may come to therapy

Session 3

When Ali arrives for this visit, he is wearing a sweater with a hood, which he has pulled up over his head. On the top of his hand he has a sticker showing a tiger with open jaws. It is not a picture of an adorable member of the cat family but rather of a beast. Perhaps the tiger gives him a feeling of protection against a threatening outer world. He pushes the hood up a little on his forehead and seems less uncommunicative and contrary today. He actually seems slightly pleased about being here.

I suspect that Ali has appreciated my definitive stance about the rules that hold for all children who come to see me. As we have seen, he has needed me to be very stern in order for him to feel enough security. And we also remember that I have made it clear to him that I am concerned about not only tame animals and nice people but also predatory animals that bite and soldiers who make war. Children with Ali's problems usually feel more accepted than they are used to when they get to hear that those who are "difficult" are also welcome here. I am moved by his somewhat surprised expression when he tries to get his mind around this idea. A quick smile flits over his face, and he looks embarrassed.

Ali has a cold today and has a runny nose most of the time. I point to a box and say:

There are tissues over there if you want one.

He shakes his head in the negative, lets his nose run and says:

I can blow my nose in my hood, and indeed he does.

The situation is tragicomic. I do not show any reactions to this stunt, but I could both laugh and cry. He knows what I think about his blowing his nose on his sweater; I can see that from his body language. But I have to choose my fights with him wisely in order to bring out some of his positive sides. My strategy is to refrain from verbally condemning all the nonsense that he comes up with, which goes against what he is expecting. If I corrected him all the time, I would not have any time left to point out his good sides. I also try to keep him in line by speaking in the imperative *before* he can succeed in his attempts to provoke me. Ali does not admit that he can need a helping hand. He answers no automatically when he is offered something, without reflecting over whether it could make things easier for him.

Ali goes over to the sand tray and sets up cars, aeroplanes and boats as well as horses and polar bears. He makes motor noises the whole time and sounds like different vehicles. He puts in all the animals imaginable until the sand tray is jammed full. He has a long line of cows, a group of horses packed together beside each other and lots of pigs clustered together in a corner. It seems like the toys are for the most part set out according to colour. He seems to like an arrangement whereby all animals of the same colour are together. I ask about the game:

What's going on?
The browns are standing there, brown horses and brown bears. All the whites are over there, polar bears and sheep. They're hanging out and waiting.

While Ali is telling me more, the piglet gets a sow for a mum and a horse for a dad. He does not know which animals belong together in an animal family. Is this possibly how his picture of his own family appears to him?

Since the sand tray is jammed with toys, the animals cannot do anything except stand and wait. Under such crowded conditions, no one can make contact with anyone else. Ali shows that he is not especially interested in seeking contact with others.

Ali talks baby talk aloud to himself. I do not hear what he is saying and it is probably not his intention for me to do so, but his tone does not sound negative. I must make myself clear:

Ali, I don't understand what you're saying but I really want to. If you also want me to understand, you need to talk in your usual way.

After Ali has told me that I am too stupid to understand anything, he starts to carry on a dialogue with the animals. He gradually gets more and more communicative, and his voice gets normal enough. He talks about what is happening to the animals. It sounds strikingly similar to such things as can happen during a boy's day at school. The animals are "learning all sorts of things". Here Ali shows that he is an alert and quick-witted boy. He counts the toys, reads the car makes and identifies colours and letters. He knows such things as seven-year-olds are expected to know. He can also show what he knows, as long as he can do it entirely on his own terms. When children have difficulties following instructions the way Ali does, they can seldom come to their right in school. Teachers have a hard time determining what they know and say about them in resignation, "They could do it if only they wanted to." However, it is not this cut-and-dried when it comes to Ali. He has the will, that is entirely certain, but he is not capable of finding the right pathways, since he gets overwhelmed by an intense inner agitation.

Since he has been speaking clearly for a while even though not directly to me, I try to go back to having a conversation:

How are things at school?

No answer. He chatters away about everything imaginable other than my question. It takes a while but then I understand that he probably wants me to guess the name of his school. When I do not start doing a lot of guessing, he shouts:

What's the matter with you? Don't you get what I mean at all?
No, actually I don't, I don't right now.

I think this is starting to be tiresome and I do not want to let him provoke me any more, so I help him stop himself:

If you want me to get what you mean, you must speak to me in an understandable way. Stop talking like that. After all, you're a big boy and a clever boy. You know I want to know what you can do. You've already shown me what you can't do.

Even if it feels like I am up against a wall of resistance, I believe that the best way to go is to support him in discovering his good sides. I do not let myself be interrupted when he starts to make noise but instead I raise my voice:

You probably don't know that you're capable of lots of things, Ali. You really are a capable boy; I can see that.

He looks like he wonders where I got this idea, but he remains silent. He naturally does not know anything about how I am used to assessing development in children, even when they are noisy and cannot concentrate. But I do not want to give up the thought that it will be possible to get Ali to discover his capabilities himself.

Ali gets up from the floor, brushes the sand off his hands and says that he has finished playing with the toys. He points at the objects and tells me:

A tow truck was gonna help another car. Maybe it had a flat tire or something. They can't figure out what's broken 'cause no one knows.

Family history

I sit still and am silent but I show my interest so that Ali will want to continue talking. The least little "wrong" comment on my part could disturb him and cause him to cease talking. This feels like a balancing act both for Ali and for me. He mumbles:

The crocodiles and the tigers are stupid. They've run away from another country. The cars get along okay 'cause they were born in the same country. The animals weren't and I wasn't either.

He pauses briefly and I wonder cautiously:

Which country do the animals come from?
They don't know. They've forgotten to ask where it was.

He points at the polar bears:

They anyhow come from Iceland.

He continues talking and I try to catch what he is really telling me behind it all. I wonder, just as cautiously this time:

How did they get to Iceland?
They got there on an animal aeroplane. The animals were passengers, like. They've run away.
Yes, of course there can be different reasons for animals to run away to another country.

Ali looks like he is considering what I am saying but he does not respond, so I ask:

What are the polar bear cubs thinking?
They don't know where they've been. Well, their mum and dad are gonna be really mad. Their mum's still in Iceland. Their mum and dad lived there. They were born there.

I venture to ask, almost in a whisper:

How do the cubs feel?
Feel? Yeah, they feel for each other.
And how do you think that smallest cub feels, deep down inside?
Not good.
Do you think the animals are sorry they've run away from their country?
Yeah, answers Ali.
How did that happen?
They were supposed to go to another part of Iceland 'cause they weren't allowed to stay on the iceberg.
Are they longing to go back, do you think, Ali?
The mum was born in Sweden and in Iceland. Stupid, isn't it?
And the dad?

No answer so I let that question drop. I want to hear more about the other animals since Ali so clearly identifies with their story.

Where is home for the animals?

Ali answers while he points at the sand tray:

There, not on Iceland. The mum said it was dangerous there but it wasn't.

He could not communicate his thoughts about his mum's and his own origins more clearly than this. I say:

The mum probably didn't know that it could be dangerous in the new country. But it must be hard for the cubs to understand all that. But polar bear mums want to protect their cubs and usually take them to a place they believe is safe.

Ali blinks and listens as I say:

When grown-ups don't know who's going to be nice and who's going to be nasty, it's really hard for their children to know that.

No answer. Ali's nose is not running any more. He sits still and turns his empty trouser pockets in and out. He starts to fiddle with a crocodile that is lying in the toy cupboard. It has open jaws and displays rows of sharp, pointed teeth. Ali describes the crocodile's lot:

It's one of a kind. It's got nowhere to belong. There are no more like him, says Ali, despite the fact that there are more crocodiles on the shelf behind him.

That the crocodile has nowhere to belong reflects Ali's own sense of being an outsider. He is starting to get tired now and takes a big yawn. Before it occurs to him that he has been entirely too willing to talk, I hasten to toss in a comment:

That crocodile looks ferocious, but it also seems to feel lonely and a little scared.
How do you see that? Ali retorts sharply.
From the teeth and the eyes, is my answer. *It's always good to look at the faces of both animals and people. Then we can see if they're going to be nice or angry.*

Assessment on his own terms

Ali does not want to say more but instead parks the cars in long rows. I still do not want to give up hope when it comes to carrying out some of the test tasks that I had planned to include in the assessment. To this end I take out a test that consists of pictures of animals in various everyday situations, and I ask him to tell about them. He refuses. I try another test, where I suggest that he draw a person but I am not able to interest him in that either. He says quite simply no, and it stays that way. I abandon further attempts with these tasks, which I really had wanted to carry out. The results of these tests can normally provide many clues about the reasons behind a child's feelings and thoughts. But I will have to draw my conclusions about these matters based on my clinical experience of psychological assessment. Children who are not able to carry out these test tasks are usually, like Ali, afraid of exploring their own feelings.

Ali is sitting still so I go on with the conversation:

Do you draw very much at home?
Yes, but I only draw when Granddad died. They didn't let my mum go to the funeral. She was little when he died. She couldn't behave herself.

In reality Aisha's father died shortly before Ali was born, but I make no comment on that. I want to hear Ali's fantasies about his granddad. I stay on the theme of death and funerals:

Sometimes grown-ups don't get the chance to be at a funeral either, even though they want to very badly, I say, and I think about what Aisha has told me. *Children aren't always allowed to go to a funeral. The grown-ups think it'll make the children too unhappy. It's not because the children are badly behaved that they don't get to be there. Children never misbehave at a funeral. The ones who usually misbehave get serious. All children can get serious.*

Ali says quietly:

I wish he's alive.

Of course Ali has never met his grandfather, but it sounds as though his memory is kept alive in Ali's and Aisha's home. I get a feeling that Ali in his inquiring way would like to talk to me about his family's home country and history but that he is not able to formulate the important questions. Who is alive? Who is dead? What is taboo to mention? He avoids saying anything about his dad but tells me:

When the New Year comes, we get to make a wish. I wish he's gonna be alive.

Ali speaks as though this could happen in the present time because he most likely has not given up his grandfather, despite everything. He expresses a vague desire that much of what has been done could preferably have remained undone. Many things that have affected his life remain wrapped in mystery. This is true of his own background and of what his mother has experienced. The fact is that he knows extremely little about his home country and its history.

Before we end I suggest:

If you want to, you can bring some drawings from home with you next time. I would really like to see some.

I do not get any response because when Ali opens the door, he bumps his head on the doorframe. It does not really look like it is only an accident. He does not show any reaction to the pain that he inevitably must feel so I say:

Ouch! Now your forehead hurts.

He responds by rubbing his head. Ali lets me follow him to the waiting room today without any objections. Aisha gives me a worried look as she asks me how things have gone today. I defer to Ali to let him answer and he shrugs his shoulders and says, "good". I agree. We say that Ali is coming here for the last time next week, and I remind them about the drawings.

Session 4

Ali has two drawings from home with him. He digs around in his mum's bag and snatches them up. We say bye to her and she goes to the waiting room. Ali has drawn trees and robots.

One for dad and one for mum. Dad's gonna get his some other day. Or maybe . . .

The chance of giving his dad a drawing remains hanging in the air. There is a great difference in quality between the two drawings. An outside observer could believe that they have been drawn by two different boys. This shows that Ali's performance capability varies depending on his state of mind. He has also brought along a game that he has created himself. It consists of small bits of paper in various colours and a larger piece of paper on which he has drawn dragons and "invisible" gold. He mutters to himself:

In this game you die.

I really want to look at the game, and he shows it to me quickly. He rattles off rules that are as incomprehensible for him as for me. I insert:

You know, it's easier to play if both of us know some rules before the game begins.

That we can set up more than one common rule turns out to be impossible. If I were to insist on it, the whole game would end up flying off the table. I can feel it in the air. We start to "play" and Ali moves the bits of coloured paper around. I keep up with the action as well as I can. Ali does not want to make it possible for me to understand the idea with the game. We have a little verbal exchange about dragons and the treasure of gold and about how his coloured bits rush around all over the game board paper while mine move one step at a time. In order to stop everything from turning into a complete mess I say:

We have the same goal, you and I, when we play. It is to save ourselves from the evil dragons and to find the shining treasure of gold. It's hard because we can't see the gold. But we have to work hard to find good pathways.

This game arouses Ali's competitive instinct. He wants to win and indeed he does win. It is easier for Ali to talk about the goal itself than about which pathways he should choose to reach it. After the game Ali fetches some markers and makes some red streaks on a paper. He is rough and one of the markers breaks. Perhaps he is trying to draw a ladybird, since he says:

There's a ladybird and it got broken.

At this point I am finally able to interest him in drawing:

If you want to, you can draw a new ladybird. There are more red markers.

He seems to be under a strain and stands broad-legged on the floor in order to have control of the situation while he draws with a blue marker. He draws something that looks like a blue ladybird with green spots. He tries out the various markers while he talks and he is turned toward me. When I do not understand what he says, he clarifies things. It is touching to see how he struggles with himself to avoid saying something rude to me.

I talk to Ali about how it is hard for him to do something that other people want him to do. He responds by seating himself under the table and making loud noises. He complains that one of his ears hurts.

Well, maybe it's not such a good idea to make all that noise if your ear hurts. And if you do that, you can't hear what I'm saying and I think you want to hear it.

Ali, Dad and Granddad

To avoid the subject of noise and listening, Ali tells me about the tree he has drawn for his dad:

He wants people to leave him alone.

This is most likely what Ali feels about his father. It can seem to Ali that he has withdrawn and does not want to have anything to do with his son. As if in response to my thoughts he says:

And so do I.
Well, sometimes I'm sure you want to be left alone. It's not the same thing, though, to want to be left alone as to feel lonely. Sometimes people say they want to be left alone because they don't have anyone to be with. I think you need some practice in how to ask other children if you can play with them.

I stay for a while on the theme of the difference between choosing to be alone versus being forced to do so. He is listening so I continue:

I understand that you want us to talk to each other. But there are many people who don't understand that you want to talk to them when you talk in that strange voice. They don't understand what's going on at all when a big boy, who can even speak two languages, speaks in such an odd way.

A quick grin passes over Ali's face. When we have finished talking about Ali's style of speech, he tells me that he has a computer at home that has belonged to his granddad. He tries in every way he can to make his granddad a part of his daily life. Or is it his dad? During this conversation he takes a little fire-breathing dragon out of his pocket. I express interest in this creature:

May I please see it?
I don't know what kinda dragon it is. You gotta ask my dad. He knows everything.

Ali sounds slightly desperate when he says I should ask his dad. However, it does not occur to him that his dad and I do not have a common language since he himself can switch so easily between Swedish and Arabic.

There's only one thing Dad doesn't know and that's how there can be more and more of something. You gotta go to some brain trust to find that out.

I listen intently in order to understand what he is actually trying to tell me and he continues:

I think it gets empty in a milk carton. Why's it full when you buy it? Milk's like everything else imaginable; it's full, and it gets to be more and more.
Well, okay.

Ali has brought up the subject of his father, and this seems to have made him confused. He goes on:

Sometimes there's just empty stuff. In Africa a three-year-old can't grow up. But sometimes there are only grown-ups like in Sweden. And in Africa there are only children.

Still perplexed, I insert:

Okay. So that's the way you think about it.

I need a little time for reflection so that I can catch the message in what he is saying. Is he illustrating his own feelings? Sometimes they overflow, without his knowing where they come from, and sometimes perhaps he feels emptiness inside himself? Or perhaps he is making associations with the fear of lacking food or other nourishment? Has Aisha had such experiences and has Ali heard about them? Is he wondering about his own chances of growing up? Ali is probably talking about things that he has somehow absorbed without understanding how they are connected.

His tone becomes somewhat softer as our conversation progresses, and he says to me as if to find out what I think:

I'd like to be a big brother, well anyhow never a big sister.

Perhaps this comment implies a question about whether he has any siblings. Perhaps he believes that I have the answer to that question.

I hate girls 'cause they're such crybabies. If I fall down I never cry. Tears are ugly.

Since I do not agree I say:

Tears come to our eyes so that we can cry them. You know, sometimes something makes us sad or we hurt ourselves.
Not me.

Now Ali thinks we have said enough about feeling sad. I maintain my earlier impression that behind his facade Ali is a sensible boy who makes himself look bad, without understanding what he is doing. He has absorbed lots of things but cannot arrange his experiences in a logical order.

We talk more about his dad, and he says:

He drinks a lot, but nothing. Kids at school talk about their dads. Dad this, Dad that. Dad can fall down.

I say:

I notice that you think a lot about your dad.

He answers with emphasis:

Yep.

I wonder to myself if Ali means that his dad falls down when he has drunk alcohol. Aisha has not said anything about this, and I do not ask further questions. It is as though Ali senses what I am thinking because he is on guard the whole time. While Ali is talking about his dad, he stretches a rubber band that he has found on the floor and aims it at me. It seems as though he senses that I trust him not to shoot the rubber band at my face. Nonetheless, I say:

Take that thing away! I can't concentrate on what I'm going to answer if you do that. I don't like it.

He puts the band aside and instead pulls off one of his socks to show me that he has a wart on the sole of his foot. He raises his foot and I inspect it. We talk about how it is good that his mum has bought some medicine to take away the wart.

Ali is more communicative at this session, but on his own terms, of course. He says what he wants to say and indicates when he wants me to be quiet. I listen gladly to what he tells me and do not ask especially many questions. He feels surer of himself when he leads the conversation and I listen. I show that I am curious about him, just like I think he has come to be about me, at least a little bit. Words and sentences flow out of him. Everything is connected to his family's history.

He talks to himself with a clear and distinct voice while he plays with the animals:

The animals have run away or have been kidnapped from another country. There are mums and dads who've been left all alone. They're mad as hell. Only things that are born in the same country can make it. I'm never Swedish 'cause I wasn't born in the same country. The ones who're left behind are mad as hell at the ones who ran away in the war.

He comes out with many long and complicated sentences, all having a similar content. He does not seem to see any way out of his dilemma of "not belonging". There is no sign of a present time or a future time in his games, only a past time that he does not understand.

I have written down some of my thoughts in a notepad during the sessions. He is interested, flips a little through my papers and asks:

Have you filled this whole list with stuff about me?
Yes, I have!

He calls the lined paper a list.

I write stuff down because I want to remember what you build in the sand tray and what we talk about. I think it's important.

This seems to confuse Ali. I continue:

I write down what you know and can do as well as things you need help with.

He answers:

I can count up to 109 but then it's over.
Wow, you can count lots of numbers. Can you write any letters of the alphabet?

I ask him these questions because here toward the end I want him to have a chance to show me things he knows.

Ali answers by writing MUM, DAD, ALI.

Great that you're showing me what you know. That's exactly what I want to see. Now I see that I've been right about you all along, that you're actually a clever kid.

Time goes fast this session, and when time is up, Ali is surprised that he must go. I hold up four fingers to show how many times we have met. Ali responds by giving me the finger, but lets me take hold of the finger. I bend it down while I say jokingly:

Listen up, you clever kid. One finger means only one and didn't you say you can count to 109?

Ali gives me a quick smile and lets me have my way.

I end the session by underscoring once again that I have noticed he can do lots of things and knows a lot, but that he cannot always show it. I also say that I notice he has a hard time doing what others tell him to do. This is something he has to practice on a lot, especially now when he is going to start at a new school. I talk about the importance of doing as his teachers say. They are the ones who know how it is supposed to be at school, and they are the ones who have to make final decisions. They are responsible for making a good environment for the children. Ali wants to get away from the theme and says:

Sometimes we get to decide in the afternoon.

It sounds like you have a nice teacher.

When I say that we have met for the last time, Ali looks straight at me and wonders why. He has been told that we would meet four times because I wanted to see if I could understand more about why it is sometimes hard for him to meet others halfway, why he often wants to have everything his own way. I also mention some other difficulties that his mum described in the introductory talk. I remind him that his mum is waiting for him in the waiting room and say:

I'll go with you. I want to talk to your mum about making an appointment to meet so that I can tell her what we've done and what I think.

Is this a mum? Ali asks me this and picks up a babushka with smaller identical babushkas inside it.

Yes, she can be a doll mum.

As a response Ali deliberately drops the doll on the floor so that all the smaller doll pieces are scattered all over the room. While he watches, I put all the parts together so that the babushka is whole again and I say in conclusion:

A broken mum can become a whole mum again.

Ali needs all the reinforcement he can get to bolster his hopes for healing, both for mums and children. Everything can be mended. Aisha brightens up and smiles at Ali when we enter the waiting room. She clearly loves her son, even though she does not always have the stamina to be the ever-ready mother she so passionately wishes she could be.

Ali's psychic health

There is much I want to talk to Aisha about based on the results of the assessment, so we meet three times. Ali's uncle Hamid, who also feels responsible for his nephew, joins us for the third meeting. Aisha's request has been for me to limit myself in this book to writing about the results I have obtained by means of the assessment. She has asked me not to go into detail about the talks that she and I have had. The following is a summary of my findings and of what I have presented to Aisha and Hamid.

Ali is seven years old when he comes in for a psychological assessment at the advice of his school. He does not know why he is coming, so I tell him why children usually come to see me. During the first visit he struggles to ignore me and does not show me his face. He has his cap pulled down over his forehead. He immediately shows me the negative image he has of himself when he explains that he does not want to take off his cap "cause it's so ugly if I do". He is in attack mode, provocative and rude, everything to live up to the negative view he has of himself. Even though he is only a little child, Ali gives an impression of being unapproachable. To protect himself, he initially fends off my attempts to communicate with him.

My spontaneous impression, which is reinforced as time goes on, is that Ali bears an inner pain that is entirely too intense for a boy his age. It is particularly striking during the first visits that Ali does not have any acceptable ways of showing his thoughts and his feelings. He has great difficulties answering, adapting and accepting help. He does not know what to do with himself. He distorts his voice, making it impossible to understand him. He refuses to carry out such test tasks as children in general enjoy doing, tasks which make it possible to understand their psychic suffering more easily. Ali does not dare to let down his guard in the beginning or tell me anything about himself or his mother. Instead, he maintains a condescending and provocative attitude. He does everything he can to make me feel like a rubbish pile. There is something deeply moving about this seven-year-old boy. I think about him even after my work is finished for the day.

Ali tries desperately to take command, and he asserts his right to decide no matter what. He does so regardless of whether or not there is anything to decide. Much of Ali's psychic energy is expended on kicking down doors that are already open. Toward the end of the first session Ali does harm to me physically. When I hold on to his arm to stop him, he roars out that I am hitting him and shouts pleadingly for help. He needs a clear setting of limits in order to understand that this stunt or similar ones will get him nowhere. He is looking for limits, and when he receives a forceful and unequivocal framework for his behaviour, he calms down. He does not seem to have much experience of meeting resistance.

He shows how he feels inside through his games, where he breaks up and destroys everything, leaving only chaos. My impression is that he is staging his own life history, which is wrapped in mystery. He has an unusual manner of sometimes identifying with the good, and sometimes with the evil, when he plays war. He cannot choose sides since he must have control over everything and everyone. The objects in his games are taken up by a whirlwind for the most part, and he cannot distinguish between his impulses, thoughts and feelings. The response that he is quickest to exhibit is aggressivity, which gives him short-term satisfaction. He shows that he thinks a lot about his origins and his biological father. In his games he combines animal mums and their children with dads belonging to other species of animals.

Ali shows in many ways that he needs both psychic and physical security in the form of a consistent setting of limits by the adult world. Adults can thereby take responsibility for him and treat him like the schoolboy he is, now that he has started his first year of school. It appears that he harbours a feeling of terror in the face of an unexpected catastrophe. In his games soldiers kill people who are sitting peacefully in their own homes. There is no protection for them. In addition to being afraid of external threats, Ali is most certainly also terror-stricken in the face of his own sudden outbreaks of aggression. He does not know how any of these things can be kept under control, no matter how he tries.

Ali comes more and more to his right during the latter part of the assessment. After much flexibility, encouragement and perseverance on my part, he begins to understand that I also want to see his ordinary and positive sides. He stops his hysterical fooling around, and his defiance fades away for long spans of time. To get to this point, Ali needed to see that his provocations were not going to be allowed to take the upper hand in our meetings. I showed him that I do the best I can for all of the children who come to see me, regardless of whether they are "naughty or nice".

Ali becomes more and more communicative and easier to like after I have shown my interest several times in animals and dolls in his games that bite and kill others. Even if it takes place for the most part on his terms, words and sentences flow out of his mouth while he plays. He stages his own story with the help of the animals and it seems to be without context. He speaks in a clear and distinct voice so that I can get an idea of the chaos that reigns – of animals that run away, get kidnapped and taken to another country; of mums and dads that are abandoned and furious.

If I look beyond Ali's attitude, I note that he, despite everything, is a quick-witted boy with good general knowledge and a large Swedish vocabulary. According to his mum, he is equally good at Arabic. He is completely up to age level when it comes to things that seven-year-olds are expected to know. He must have absorbed knowledge in preschool even though his teachers have not believed that he did. However, he puts it entirely in my hands to use all my perseverance in order to coax forth and get a view of his talents. Ali can do many things and knows a lot, but he does nothing on his own to show these things since he is so unsure about them. He does not realize how, when and why he should show anyone these things. Because of his easily awakened anxiety, he does not always seem to have access to his knowledge when he needs it. Despite his considerable talent, he mixes up the real and the unreal.

What, then, is at the basis of Ali's difficulties? They are of such a magnitude and nature that we can suspect their causes to be found partly in the early years of his life. Ali was born in a foreign country to a mother who was a single parent and frightened. She did not know that she was pregnant when she came to Sweden. She has told me that she has been deeply depressed. Such factors naturally have consequences for the development of the relationship between mother and child, especially if the depression remains over time and if there are no others within the family who have a close relationship to the child. Aisha did not get any help with her son in the early years, and he was a lively child from the very beginning.

Aisha's condition has improved as the years have gone by, but she still has periods of depression and anxiety. She struggles to forget the experiences that have traumatized her. According to my judgement, she has suffered from and is still suffering from the condition known as post-traumatic stress disorder, or PTSD. Her problems have thus been present during Ali's entire life. PTSD is a serious and well-known condition in traumatized people. I talk to Aisha at length about the good therapeutic help that is available and that can alleviate her symptoms. I hope that our talks can motivate her to seek help for herself as well.

Aisha suffers from guilt feelings for her depression and says that it has contributed to her inadequacy as a mum. She means that she has not had the stamina to give Ali consistent love. She sees this as the root of her son's problems. However, I am not prepared to agree with her entirely when she says that her depression could indirectly explain all of Ali's anxiety and agitation. He has the types of themes in his play that children usually have when they are staging some unspoken "family secret". It is never talked about in the home, but it hovers around there as something vaguely threatening. Children know inside themselves that this "something" is not possible to talk about, but they express it indirectly in their games. I get a definite feeling that in his fantasies Ali is reliving and suffering anxiety from his mum's memories of her trauma. The contexts are just as incomprehensible for him as they are for Aisha. He does not know why frightful themes keep turning up in his games or why his games come to incomprehensible ends. Aisha does not understand that her memories from the time before Ali was even born have been able to affect him.

Ali has tried, despite his young age, to take over the responsibility for his little family, partly because that is what children try to do if the only parent they have does not function fully well and partly because, as Aisha says, that is what is expected of a son in her culture. Mother and son must struggle to bring about a change. We say that Aisha must gather the stamina to take back her parent role, and Ali must get back into the child role. Aisha has not believed that her son has had any special thoughts about their background, since he has never asked any questions. She is strongly touched when she hears that Ali shows his confusion so clearly and that so much of his psychic energy is spent on trying to understand his and her life in his fantasies. Aisha wonders how I can draw my conclusions, so I tell her about Ali's chaotic war games with good and evil, in which he does not know which side he wants to belong to. I assure Aisha that I have met many children whose parents have experienced different traumas. I therefore recognize such reactions in children well, despite not knowing exactly what has happened to the families.

Aisha is naturally unhappy and worried about what I tell her. At the first meeting she is shocked but she looks considerably more resolute at the second one, and at the third one her brother Hamid comes along. They both feel urgency for Ali to get professional help but they also want to understand how they themselves can help him. Ali's ability to relate to me has gradually improved as he and I have got to know each other. This is a positive sign for his future social development. Beginning to dare to initiate and accept contacts with others is the first step in building up trusting relationships. Ali is going to need reliable and durable relationships to several people, not just to his mum.

When we are joined by Hamid, our conversation turns to war experiences, but only in general terms. Both of them are of the conviction that they must spare their children knowledge of such things. I share their conviction. Without knowing the specifics of Aisha's trauma, I talk to them about how the two of them need to help each other determine how much they can tell Ali in order to reduce his anxiety and provide answers to his unspoken questions. Whatever happens, they need to be keenly alert to his reactions and questions and be as open as they can about the consequences of war. Hamid is of the opinion that Iraqi children see too much on television about the situation in Iraq. He is entirely right when he says that children from Iraq must be assured that we have peace in Sweden, the country where they are living.

I suggest to Aisha that she contact a child and adolescent psychiatric clinic when they have moved to the new town. She needs a lot of support to muster the energy to shift Ali's attitude. He is scared of his lack of ability to control himself. This makes it impossible for him to steer his behaviour. He needs his mum's continued love but also her predictable and stable limit-setting, which give him protection. I talk about how important it is for a lively boy who grows up with only his mum to receive both unconditional love and limits from her in particular. In that way, the risk that the child will take out his frustrations on his mum later in life is avoided. Aisha asks at one point if I mean that she should be "nice but firm". Yes, that is exactly what I mean.

Aisha and Hamid should also get in touch with the new school. Ali will most certainly need extra support, and maybe they should ask to have him put in a class with fewer pupils so that he can identify what he is good at as well as what he does not know yet. It is necessary for Ali to get a stable platform for the future development of his identity. But Aisha also puts a lot of hope in Hamid because with him Ali is a different boy. It is obvious that Hamid and Ali like each other a lot. Hamid concludes by saying that he has not understood that Ali does not know his own capabilities. He intends to encourage him when he does things well so that he will realize what is good.

I hope that the psychological assessment has given Ali and his mother the belief that there are possibilities for both of them to go forward. Ali has received a taste of what it is like to be understood and seen as the person he is. Aisha dares to acknowledge that her son is having a hard time and that it is not only at school that things are not going well. She intends to seek more psychological help for him and no longer sees it as something shameful.

Twelve years later

I have thought about Ali now and again over the years and wondered how things have turned out for him. Twelve years after I saw him last, I suddenly see him standing right in front of me as I prepare to leave a lecture hall. I have just held a lecture in his town. His mum had seen my name in the announcement for the lecture and had told him. So he has been sitting here and listening as I have spoken about children with the diagnosis of ADHD (attention deficit hyperactivity disorder). He asks if I recognize him and smiles from ear to ear when I actually do. I ask him how he is doing, and he really wants to tell me so we go and sit down in a cafeteria. Ali says that he does not remember much from our meetings, but his mother definitely does. One thing he does remember is how he ran up and down stairs that never seemed to end. Ali tells me that his mum had an awakening, so to say, after their visits with me. She has told him that it was not until then that she understood what a hard time he was having. This became a turning point for both of them.

Regarding his school years, he admits that he drove some of his teachers "crazy". There were years he attended classes with a smaller number of pupils than the standard. That was fine with him because he got more help that way. He has now graduated from upper secondary school with such good results that he has been accepted into the university programme of his choice.

"Things got a lot better when we moved away from Stockholm, so it wasn't just me and mum cooped up in a tiny flat," Ali continues. There are many people who have helped him, both Uncle Hamid and various teachers. "A neighbour named Gösta has really stood by me," says Ali emphatically. "He kept at me about not doing idiotic stuff. He had just retired when we became neighbours, so he had time and he liked me for some reason. He had messed up a lot as a kid, too." Ali has spent a lot of time with Gösta over the years, tinkering about with his antique car. That car was the apple of Gösta's eye, so if Ali started fooling around in the garage Gösta made him leave. He slaps his knees and laughs contentedly when he says that Gösta "could give me a hell of a telling off", but that he also defended Ali many times. Ali has never wanted to disappoint Gösta since he has believed in him wholeheartedly all these years. Ali acknowledges that he has a lot to thank Gösta for. Without him Ali would not be where he is today.

Ali has been to Iraq once to visit his dad. He found out then that the man in question was not his biological father. He was not surprised, as he had always suspected this to be the case. During a certain period of time Ali tried to find out who his biological father was. But he met obstacles wherever he turned, and people just shook their heads. Aisha had asked him to stop looking. He just makes a quick comment to the effect that women fare badly in all wars and then it is up to them to take care of the consequences. I nod and understand that the subject is closed.

The conversation goes on for a long time and is rewarding for both of us. We do not get out of our seats until the cafeteria is about to close. It has warmed my heart to sit and listen to Ali, who, from having been a badly behaved little boy with a huge burden on his shoulders, has become a sharp and handsome young man of nineteen years who wants to share what he has accomplished in life. I am touched and impressed as I give him a pat on the arm, remembering how I thought that the seven-year-old Ali needed to realize what was good about him so that he could show it. This the nineteen-year-old Ali has clearly accomplished.

I send a greeting to Aisha, who is working the night shift at the hospital's surgical ward. We bid farewell and I wish Ali all the best in his studies. When we part ways I think with joy about Gösta and the male role model he has become for a boy who so desperately needed one. The world would need many more Göstas. I am also delighted that the psychological assessment helped Aisha find the stamina to work through her son's and her own issues.

Traumatic experiences of parents

Reactions to difficult traumas that remain un-worked-through in the parent generation can be transferred to coming generations, thus onto yet unborn children. This is true not only for large-scale traumas of a national character, such as war experiences or natural catastrophes, but also for private traumas that have taken place in the unborn child's family. A number of studies have shown that even though a parent may never have touched on his or her experienced trauma consciously, residual memory images can be transferred to children and bring about negative consequences for their psychic well-being.

The emotionally strong links between little children and their parents make children extremely in tune with their parents' unspoken states of mind and needs. If a child is kept in the dark about overwhelmingly severe experiences his mum or dad has had in the past, his relationship to that parent can meet with difficulties. This is particularly true if something frightful can be sensed in the home atmosphere. That traumatized people keep silent about their experiences and by doing so attempt both to hide and to forget is a common phenomenon. For Ali's mum, not telling anyone about what she had experienced in her war-torn home country had an immediate survival value.

Children are extremely loyal to their parents, particularly if the parents are not functioning optimally. Children and parents also protect each other when there are unspoken secrets, large as well as small. They share a tacit agreement that there is something in the family that is impossible to talk about. The child does not want to pester the parents with questions and the parents in their turn think the child knows nothing or is not interested. After having talked to many children of traumatized parents, my experience is partially the opposite. In every family there are things, major as well as minor, that the members do not want to announce to the world but would rather keep within the walls of the home and therefore do not talk about. But many children, who do not know exactly what the whole thing is about, show in a psychological assessment that they are harbouring incomprehensible fantasies that are terrifying and threatening to them.

Children both want and do not want to know what has happened since they have accurately understood that it is something terrifying in the extreme. Since everything is so incomprehensible, children often think this unknown thing can happen again completely without warning. In the case of a trauma specific to one time in the past, children need to be assured that it will not happen again. In reality, it is over and *only thoughts* about what happened live on. Granted, it does not feel entirely right to use the expression "only thoughts" in this context. Nonetheless, it is important for children to get help so they can distinguish between the adult's thoughts on the one hand and their own fantasies on the other.

We usually assert that children's own fantasies often make things look worse than what has happened in reality and therefore cause them anxiety. But when it comes to war experiences, children's fantasies fall short. Reality in the case of war is worse. The parent is trying not to show his or her suffering within the family, and so the child tries to keep things to himself as well. He does not want to burden an already hard-pressed parent but instead tries to shoulder adult responsibilities that are beyond his maturity. Many traumatized parents are also incapable of seeing that the child has problems that must be taken seriously. Everything seems of minor importance compared to what they have gone through, which in a purely factual sense is true. But both in the short- and long-term, the child's development is affected in a negative manner. Oftentimes it is teachers who must make parents aware of the child's problems. The problems can take the shape of the child's identifying with the parent's history and the parent's reactions of hate and dread because people have deliberately degraded and violated him or her. The child does not know which people might be to blame for his feelings of catastrophe and therefore strikes out rather randomly at individuals in his surroundings. During my meetings with Ali, he shows clearly that he responds to other people with impulse breakthroughs.

A parent's un-worked-through experiences, which have led to a general psychic weakness and depression, undermine the stability in the relationship to the child. Ali's mother, who did not receive enough help to come out on the other side of her experiences, did the best she could for her son. She gave him love but did not always have the stamina to set limits that were secure enough for him. If a trauma has done so much harm to a parent, it also affects the child's psychic health. Ali's mother received the diagnosis PTSD, post-traumatic stress disorder. This is the medical diagnosis made when a person has experienced physical and/or psychological threats and thereafter displays symptoms such as a terror-stricken and recurrent reliving of the experience. She tries desperately to escape thoughts of the trauma without succeeding, which triggers extreme anxiety.

Children can function as though they have this diagnosis themselves if they have been marked by the experiences that are psychically alive in the home. No one understands, though, that these symptoms are the after-effects of a trauma in the past. In the child's fantasies something ghastly can happen again. The child feels fearful of the world around him, but the aggressive impulses that come from inside him are what usually scare him the most. Therefore, the child avoids such things as are unknown and that could reveal that he harbours feelings other than aggressive ones. Ali does what many children do in similar situations. He avoids all test tasks that concern feelings. He does not want to show any weakness since that could trigger anxiety. And how would his little family manage if both he and his mum were shown to be weak?

When we are going to make a psychological assessment of children of traumatized parents, we must know some things about the child's background in order to best understand the reasons for his problems. But if a parent is not capable of talking about all the difficult issues, we have to respect this circumstance. In such cases I usually ask the parents to share with me those things about the child's background that they think are necessary for me to know in order to understand the reasons and causal connections behind the child's persisting symptoms.

Like Ali's mum, many assert that it is difficult to tell Swedish people about their war experiences. They most certainly have every right to feel this way. How can we, who have not experienced war, stand hearing about human evil? What can we understand? Different cultural views also make it difficult for parents born in other countries to share with us. Something I have heard not infrequently is the following. People who have been violated and tormented and beyond any doubt have been victims can still harbour feelings of shame and guilt, despite everything. The Swedish listener seems unable to understand that they can have such strong feelings of guilt as to make them unable to talk about what happened. Such feelings should belong to the perpetrator one would think, but it is considerably more complicated than that. It is an ordeal for traumatized people to be met with such reactions.

Some people who suffer from post-traumatic stress disorder recover on their own thanks to the healing power of time. Others need psychotherapeutic treatment by a specially trained trauma therapist. A successful PTSD treatment leads to a type of reconciliation with one's own fate. This helps trauma-stricken people to function better. They do not need to use so much of their energy to try to forget. In this way they can be strengthened in their parenting role and thus can prevent the symptoms from being transferred to the next generations. This, if anything, is a strong reason for Aisha to get a chance to undergo psychotherapy with a trauma therapist. Such a treatment provides good help even if it is started several years after the trauma occurred.

5 Sharing narratives about child patients

Is that acceptable?

Ethical considerations and practical advice

In this book I have described psychotherapeutic treatments with four children – Ali, Olga, Ronia and Malte – one of them from the perspective of a psychologist in supervision with me. The brief crisis interventions have led the children forward in their development and/or helped them to work through traumas in their pasts. I have wrestled with many thoughts and feelings before daring to open the closed door of my psychotherapy room to the general public. Here I would like to take up some of these feelings and thoughts. I have devoted a great deal of time to considering the possibility of publishing confidentiality-classified material about children. Would it be professionally right? Legally possible? Ethically defensible?

As far as the professional side is concerned, I have received a great deal of support and constructive criticism from many colleagues. This feedback has been indispensable for proceeding with the planning of the book. At a clinic or an institution for child and adolescent psychiatry, we work as a team around our young patients. This means that I cannot simply describe my own work without touching upon or telling about my colleagues' work. Perhaps they have had talks with the parents of a child whom I have had in therapy, and in such cases they also need to agree to let their work come into the public domain. In my experience, when I have asked my colleagues for their permission they have been happy to give it. I will take up the legal aspects later and give examples of contracts and agreements that stipulate what may be published.

It is an important question whether it is ethically defensible to publish information about children's psychic reactions and symptoms, especially when they are caught up in such vulnerable positions as portrayed in this book. Many sensitive issues have come into focus. The main one has been to understand and assess the permission given to me by mature child patients and parents of all patients to write about them and their children. Their decisions must be well considered. I have therefore carried out discussions with them about the implications that published material might have for them, lest irrelevant factors might play too great of a role.

For example, there is a risk that parents might give their permission out of gratitude for a successful treatment of their child. It can also seem exciting for a child or for parents to see themselves as the main characters in a book, but the adults must be given responsibility for foreseeing the consequences. They must also be able to imagine how siblings and other relatives are going to react.

These questions have been important, since my desire has been to write authentic narratives about children in psychotherapy. The intention has been to make my writing accessible to different groups of readers. Needless to say, the narratives are directed to those who have a professional interest in reading about children's psychic health, but I am equally keen on sharing my experiences with a broader circle of readers. I asked myself if it would be possible to reach out to both groups with the same narratives. I knew that, if so, I would need to avoid professional terminology, which at first seemed difficult. However, I started to write, determined to deal with the terminology issue as the book developed. Such terminology facilitates communication between colleagues to a great degree, but it can be an obstacle when addressing readers who do not share the writer's professional background.

I began by purchasing most of the ten bestselling books at the bookstores. I then spent several weeks lying in a hammock reading. I wanted to gain insight into what readers in general appreciated the most. All of the books were mysteries and thrillers. It became obvious that many people are keen to read exciting books with such a great measure of excitement that their curiosity is sustained throughout the entire story.

A mystery often starts out with a number of incomprehensible, seemingly unrelated events. And a good mystery conveys such a feeling of excitement that the reader wants to keep turning the page to look for more clues. He knows that the clues will shed light on whatever is mystifying. Every mystery writer sustains the hope that a solution is going to be possible. The reader thus remains convinced that he or she is gradually going to understand events and relationships that previously seemed incomprehensible. After having read only a couple of these books, I was made aware that mystery writers and psychologists have a great deal in common.

To begin putting together the puzzle of causes that have led to the manifestation of a child's psychic problems is every bit as exciting as following the plot of a mystery, from the beginning to the ending. The same ingredients as are found in a mystery novel are part of the child psychologist's work. Our excitement and curiosity are awakened with every new meeting with children and their parents. What has happened, what can we find out, how can we help?

We start by trying to piece together a picture of the child's life history and of how his or her psychic symptoms can be related to it. We psychologists know how to be patient while we work on discovering yet unmapped causal relationships. We work as hard as we can to make connections and arrive at clarity. We sustain hope up to the very end of the last therapy session just as the mystery writer does to the last page of the mystery novel. When we meet traumatized children who have lost hope of ever being happy again, it is our task to function as a source of hope until the children's own sense of hope returns.

Many people find it hard to read about children with severe problems. The text must therefore be written so that it holds the reader's interest until the child's last meeting with the psychologist has been described. Just as in a mystery story, we must often arrive at the conclusion first before we see that the child's psychic wounds have been transformed into healed scars. My ambition has been to instil the same feeling of hope into the readers of my books as into my patients. In contrast to all the mentioned similarities, there is a striking difference between writers of mystery novels and writers of psychological case studies: psychologists focus on people's *inner* processes while mystery novelists often write about *outer* events.

My discovery of these similarities strengthened my belief that narratives about inner healing processes in children should also interest a wider circle of readers. It would be an interesting challenge to write for readers without professional knowledge of child psychology.

Many readers wonder what procedures I have used to obtain permission to write about my child patients. Those of us in the care professions, such as doctors, ministers of religion, psychologists, psychotherapists and others, must act in accordance with laws of confidentiality. We are legally bound not to disclose anything that our patients or clients tell us. I will describe how I have proceeded in a later section.

My desire has been to let the reader have a close-up view and follow the psychic processes that Ali, Olga, Ronia and Malte have gone through. It is incredibly rewarding to follow such processes in a child who has suffered from traumatic experiences. Additionally, it is a stimulating challenge trying to describe the process in a written text so that subtle but important details come out fairly for each individual child. This is true when it comes to their strengths as well as their weaknesses. To put these matters into words has sometimes felt daunting. I am reminded of how difficult it is for children when their parents ask them what they have done at the psychologist's. As long as I have been a psychologist, I have never heard any parent receive a direct answer that has made him or her understand what the child has experienced during the visit that day. Putting inner development into words is every bit as complicated as it seems and requires time, maturity and reflection. The puzzled expressions on the faces of parents have provided one motivation to tell about my work with their children.

Inevitably, lots of things happen during a session when a child meets a child psychologist. These meetings cannot be compared to those with a motivated adult who has sought out a psychologist on his or her own. Adults give an account of their problems and then they talk to the psychologist about them. The adult patient and the therapist sit down in separate chairs. In contrast, children move about and change activities and themes many times during one and the same session, often at a moment's notice. They jump and bounce about or lie on the floor. They might scream, cry, laugh, converse or remain silent. Suddenly, a child needs to dash to the restroom and there is no time to lose. Neither the psychologist nor the child spends much of an extended period of time sitting down in their chairs. What usually vary between different children's therapies are the relative frequencies and lengths of these different activities. The same thing is true when it comes to the children in this book. Since children's therapy sessions are so eventful, there is always much to memorize in preparation for coming meetings.

To remember the course of the therapeutic work for the different children, I make documentation after every session. I always make a memorandum, and I usually take snapshots of the scenes children have set up or other things that have been left in the room. Since both the rhythm and the pace change often, there is not always time to grasp what is relevant while the session is actually in progress. When I read my notes afterwards, however, I often discover connections that can be useful to incorporate in the therapy on a later occasion.

Each child gets to have a box of his or her own while the therapy is in process. Everything that is saved is placed by the child or me in this box, which is private. Only the child and I are allowed to look at what is in it. There are typically drawings, paintings, little letters and other messages, clay figures and other things that the child has produced when attempting to give expression to various feelings and experiences. In Malte's case, for example, his material in the box consisted mainly of pictures and texts for the book that we made together. Ronia's box contained snapshots of the scenes she set up in the dollhouse and the sand tray. In preparation for the publication of the pictures of what the children have made, it has felt ethically correct to rearrange things somewhat, though without changing the meaning conveyed by them. The material I have saved has also provided the necessary support for my memory when I have wanted to describe some sequence in more detail.

As the reader has observed, Ali, Olga, Ronia and Malte are expressive, like most children, so there is much more that I could have written about each and every one of them. But certain themes are repeated many times with few or no variations. This can be true of recurring games or conversational exchanges. I describe such phenomena only once or twice, even though they might have occurred more often. I am pointing this out lest the reader get the impression that a child's pathway through therapy goes more directly toward the "goal" than is the case in reality. Among all the things that take place, I have selected first and foremost to write about those that have turned out to be relevant for the forward movement of the child's healing process. But I also give an account of processes that have previously held back the child's development.

Former and present family relationships for the different children are taken up in the book to the extent needed for an understanding of the conditions under which each individual child lives. These conditions might play a role in the problems that the children have at the time I meet them. When dialogues between the children and me are cited, they are given exactly as they took place in the therapy room. Nothing has been added to the narratives about the children. The real names and identities of people, places and certain circumstances have been changed. New names have been given to everything and everyone. This is true even when a child's name is mentioned indirectly in the text.

For example, in a conversation with Ronia, I commented that her mother had most likely been thinking of the character Ronia in Astrid Lindgren's book *Ronia the Robber's Daughter* when she chose her own daughter's name. In fact, her mother had chosen another name but still a name that provides the same kind of quick association to another storybook child with a forceful personality. In addition, certain information has been camouflaged in a way known only to the family involved. My routine is to choose new names in consultation with the family. Who should be named what? Who should live where? Should any relative other than the immediate family be included in the text? However, no matter how cautious I am, it is never possible to guarantee once and for all that no one who is acquainted with the family will be able to identify them.

The first step in obtaining permission to publish confidentiality-classified material is to ask for a confidentiality release from the family. I contacted a lawyer to help me draw up a contract to be used between the parents and me. All of the parents of children in this book and likewise I myself have approved and signed such a contract. The lawyer has pointed out that "the contract is valid provided that the one/the ones who have signed it are of legal age and are assumed to be able to understand the consequences of having details and scenes of therapy related to them come into publication." A written agreement of this nature protects the child, the family and the therapist. In the event that a child has divorced parents with shared custody, it is necessary for both the mother and the father to sign the contract. Permission from only one parent does not suffice.

When preparing for publication, one of the most important matters in discussions with parents is to make a spoken agreement about what should *not* be published. This holds true even if the parents, in gratitude for their child's treatment, say, "You can write whatever you want. We trust you completely." I have seen it as my responsibility in such cases to judge what, if anything, should be left out. Something might be too revealing or easy to recognize despite the camouflage. I am always completely open with the family about what I am *not* going to write about, and I explain why. By definition, such an agreement can only be made by word of mouth. If any parent has reacted with doubt about how a certain sensitive theme should be presented, I have suggested a rewording. What is put down in writing for publication must be regarded as ethically defensible by everyone involved, for all the future and regardless of who reads it.

When writing about a child, I think it is important to draw up a written agreement with the child as well, provided that he or she is mature enough and can read. None of the children in this book falls within that category. But when I have written about older children on previous occasions, I have made a written agreement with them that consists of a text in easy language. It is important for the child to feel that he or she is a part of what is going on.

The written agreement with the child is not a legally binding document. It rather concerns the ideas behind why I wanted to write about this particular child. As concerns Olga, her psychologist Jenny, on my advice, has made the written agreement with the child's parents. They were also aware that Jenny received supervision from me. We decided that Jenny would inform Olga's parents and Olga about her wish to document her therapy. Thereafter an agreement was made between Olga and Jenny. Even though Olga was ten years old at the time, we could not be certain that she completely understood the content of what she read. In any case, she received a copy of the agreement, though not signed.

Even if a child is clearly aware of everything when we are planning the writing project, he or she will forget about it after some time. At that point it can be valuable to have everything in writing. Both the child and I read the text aloud to each other. I want to make sure that he or she understands what it says. We sign our names in the presence of the parents. Sometimes I give the parents of younger children a paper like this, though not signed, that they can save until the child is older, should he or she start to wonder about the circumstances surrounding the narrative. After all, the book will surely have a place on the family's bookshelf for many years to come.

As regards younger children, who naturally cannot foresee the consequences, I always make it clear that we adults are the ones responsible for making the book or the chapter in the book a good one. I explain to the child which adults I am talking about, first and foremost the parents and myself and perhaps some other person. Needless to say, all parents have read a first draft of the text.

All individuals concerned have been given time to read and to absorb their impressions. It is always daunting to see something about one's child, oneself and one's family there on paper in black and white. None of the parents had been able to imagine beforehand how it would feel to read the text nor what strong feelings it would evoke. All were deeply moved and awed by their children when they understood how hard they had struggled to feel better and regain their joy of life. When the parents have read the text, they have shared their viewpoints with me. At this stage we have also agreed on any changes they might want to be made. The parents have often wanted me to write more about one theme or another but they have never asked to have something deleted from the text.

Formerly confidentiality-classified material, meaning material that has been released from confidentiality, requires careful treatment nonetheless. The parents have read the final version of the manuscript after all of the revisions and additions have been inserted. The contract with the parents reads, "After we have read and given our approval to the final version of the manuscript, no further revisions may be made without our consent." In other words, not even a comma may be changed at this point. The release from confidentiality given to me by the parents covers only what is written in the book. I may not give any additional details about the children or their families in other contexts outside the book.

It is a delicate matter for a psychotherapist to decide to write about certain patients and not about others. Before asking permission to publish a certain child's material, I must have convinced myself that the written material in all probability will not have an adverse effect on the child's or the family's life now or in the future. Once material has been published, it is, of course, out there forever. I talk to the parents in depth about this matter. Since I want to write as authentically as possible, I choose not to write about families in whose narrative I would need to leave out entirely too much to protect the child or the family. Needless to say, in cases where I have sensed that it would be altogether too painful for the parents to read about their child or their families, I do not even consider writing about them. Judgement in this matter rests entirely on me, regardless of whether the parents say that they are entirely willing for me to write about their child's treatment.

New patients and their parents who seek my help react in different ways to the fact that I have written about former patients. Many have read my books and comment on them. Some ask for the same therapy for their own child as the one they have read about. New technology has made it impossible for a psychologist to be as anonymous for her patients as she was in earlier times. It has become more and more common to google a person's name when preparing for a first meeting, which means that people usually know a good deal about the psychologist they are coming to see. I therefore tell new patients nowadays that my books develop in consultation with the parents of the child in therapy.

Even though the parents know it, I emphasize that I am bound by confidentiality as usual in my work with their child. I am explicit about this fact because otherwise some parents could feel too intimidated or too flattered and excited by the thought of my wanting to write about their particular child as well. In the appendices there are two examples of written agreements that I customarily use with families. The one is a contract that the parents and I have signed. The other is the agreement with underage children that I have described earlier. In such instances the child and I have read the agreement aloud together and then have signed our names on it.

My recommendation is that anyone who is considering writing about work that involves confidentiality-classified material should first discuss the matter with the head of his or her clinic or institution and afterwards consult a lawyer. My sample agreements can serve as starting points when new ones are to be drawn up. It is important that a specific contract be written up for each family, with consideration given to that particular family's situation and to the clinic or institution where the treatment has been conducted. When confidentiality-classified material from a country other than Sweden is involved, consideration must also be given to that country's laws and regulations.

A psychologist is occupied for the most part with searching for and then understanding the causes behind a child's psychic symptoms, that is, mostly negative aspects. I have therefore found it truly rewarding to have had an opportunity to examine the material on Ali, Olga, Ronia and Malte from more varying angles and especially to elucidate positive aspects that have helped these children go forward after their traumatic and tough experiences. I hope that my narratives convey the strength that children possess even in difficult situations. I also hope that I have made it clear that confidentiality laws do not necessarily always constitute an obstacle to telling about therapeutic work. I hope that this chapter has provided food for thought for anyone who wishes to share narratives about work with his or her patients or clients, whether through the spoken or the written word.

6 The child psychologist's reflections after concluded work

As previously mentioned, there is a significant difference between how adults and children express their reactions after having experienced a trauma. Adults can put words to their painful experiences and find comfort in discussing their situation with others. Adults can talk about the void left after a loss, about the horror they feel about their changed life situation and about their desperate thoughts concerning the future. Adults can understand the repercussions of traumas on an intellectual level even if they cannot accept them on an emotional level.

Children who have experienced a catastrophe, on the other hand, have a hard time talking about what has happened. They cannot put words to how they feel now and even less so to what they fear the future might hold. Young children live in the present and expect that everything will remain unchanged. They thus cannot put words to their feeling of loss about the death of a family member, for example. It is impossible for them to realize that a beloved person has disappeared forever, since fantasy and reality exist side by side in their magical world. The dead person lives on in their fantasy as if nothing has happened despite the fact that in reality she is gone. On the one hand, the child sees nothing strange or contradictory about this, while on the other hand, he or she must endure the consequences of the catastrophe.

Furthermore, many children are strongly affected by the way all the people around them look so sad and are not acting like they normally do. They like their relatives and friends as they used to be, not as they have become. However, children have to be helped to use their imagination and playfulness in order to understand and accept reality, no matter how tragic it may be. In crisis therapy we use different types of psychological tools to this end, such as playing, stories, pictures and other approaches with symbolic content.

Child psychotherapists must have a thorough knowledge of the normal psychic development in children as well as experience of how children of different ages react in crisis situations. With such theoretical knowledge serving as a base, they can then combine it with experiences from their clinical work. Theoretical knowledge also serves the therapist well as the most significant counterbalance against overidentifying with a child's tragic fate. Based on knowledge about the usual course of the working-through process after crisis reactions, the therapist can give a child hope for a good life until the family's own belief in the future returns. With that knowledge as a backdrop, it is possible to give children a measure of stability in their existence by linking their life before and after their trauma.

The therapist thus can help children dare to look back at what has happened so that they after a time will dare to start looking ahead. The therapist must have the courage to approach, together with the child, life before the trauma, the traumatic experience itself and then how life has become afterwards. Children must be made to understand that people who liked them before the trauma like them now as well. This is by no means something that children take for granted without help.

As I hope is obvious from the different narratives, work as a child psychologist is both stimulating and full of variety. The children we encounter have various psychic symptoms that manifest themselves in different ways. Some, such as Ali, have externalizing symptoms and others, such as Ronia, have internalizing symptoms. Depending on the type of symptoms, children need somewhat different approaches in their short-term therapies in order to reach a healing process.

Many think that a psychotherapist should always wait for the patient himself or herself to approach a certain theme during the therapy sessions. According to such a stance, the therapist would always be one step behind the child. But when it comes to traumatized children, the therapist needs to follow and at the same time lead the child through his or her difficult experiences. Work with an externalizing child often becomes loud and sweaty.

The therapist needs to repeat again and again in words and actions the rules and frameworks that are in place. Only then can the child calm down so that the working-through process can begin, as was the case with Ali. With these children the important task for the therapist is *to hold them in check* as they race ahead but at the same time *follow them forward* in the process. Of course, they should move forward but at a considerably calmer pace than they are used to.

With internalizing children, the working-through process is much calmer. The therapist has to *lead* these children *forward* and at the same time *keep them from going backward.* In Ronia's case it was necessary to let her move ahead at her slow, seeking pace while at the same time not letting her fall back into the old behaviour patterns she had formed over the past five years. It is never possible to speed up the inner healing process in children who are cautious in their way of expressing themselves. It is possible, however, to facilitate the process, and it is the task of the therapist to do so with this group of children. In working through traumas, it is equally important for all children, regardless of manner and disposition, to find a rhythm and a pace that are optimal. The biggest risk is having the expectation that it is going to go faster than it does. But there is never any "quick fix". If things go too fast, the child will not have time to get in touch with thoughts and feelings, thus blocking out the working-through process.

Since the ability to communicate for both children and adults breaks down in a chaotic event, it is necessary for the therapist to start out by building up a comfortable relationship with both the child and the parents. This relationship has to grow in a measured way so that the traumatized child feels trust, which is a prerequisite for the working-through process to begin. The psychotherapist also has to deal with the child at the level of development that he or she exhibits at the first meeting. Owing to the trauma, the child's development can deviate from what would be expected for a child at a certain age.

In a crisis situation, children can regress to an earlier level of development and start acting younger than their age. They can also race ahead developmentally, become precocious and act as if they were older. By realizing what the child's behaviour is a manifestation of, the therapist can determine what the true developmental level is and build up the relationship accordingly. A child's psychotherapist can quickly become a significant person not just for the child but also for the entire extended family. Everyone is relieved when the child receives help.

The therapist must also think about reacting soundly when a child in Ronia's situation starts seeking out another adult from whom to receive the care that a deceased parent earlier has given. When a child like Ronia needs physical signs of endearment, it can easily happen that she turns to her therapist with whom there is already a bond. At such a point, it is important for the therapist to make family members aware of the child's needs. Once the awareness is in place, the therapist can encourage the child to turn to these family members for extra cuddles and hugs. It can be extremely painful for the therapist to "reject" such needs, but she must avoid, for example, taking the child into her arms and hugging him or her. This avoidance can make the therapist feel like she is further "traumatizing" an already traumatized child. But we must remember that the child has started psychotherapy to work on psychological needs, and not on needs for affection. Traumatized children usually have many people around them whose welcoming arms are ready for them. We must not forget that.

While adults in crisis talk, children use play, games, fantasies and stories as natural tools when they want to *tell* what they have experienced. Adults may find it difficult to understand how playing can heal. For children, on the other hand, it is natural to see play as part of the healing process. Once I heard a four-year-old telling her dad about it: "It helps to play. I feel it all over my body." Children are keen to find different characters to identify with. In the world of stories and entertainment there is a rich variety of fictional characters and real people whom they can use thus. Children make their favourite characters' experiences into their own experiences, both real and imaginary.

Astrid Lindgren's storybook characters have helped many generations of children in difficult life situations. One example of a traumatized child is her famous character Pippi Longstocking. What can be more comforting than identifying with her? It seems reasonable to assume that Pippi has experienced many crises. Her mum is in heaven, her dad has abandoned her and she does not have any siblings. She has to keep up her guard against both bad guys and social welfare workers. Even so she lives a free and exciting life as the richest and strongest girl in the whole world – in her imagination, at least. Such a life-affirming role model as Pippi encourages children in difficult situations to work through difficulties they have experienced and regain hope of a new future.

As these children gradually begin to feel better, they develop a need to hear stories with happier endings. And for Pippi there are no problems left because everything turns out for the best. Astrid Lindgren's Emil in Lönneberga and Ronia the robber's daughter are also popular characters with whom children are keen to identify. Ronia really liked the idea that her mum had decided she would be named after the robber's daughter.

The same is true when it comes to the world famous pop star Michael Jackson. He has made it easier for many children to dare to approach existential questions that have tormented them. Where do you end up in life if you advance and yet you go backwards, too? Thoughts about racial identity and skin colour interest everyone. Can others also change skin colour, just like Michael did? His name even starts off conversations about parenthood. How do children come to the world, and who gave birth to them if there is no mum in the picture? Where did the mum go if we cannot see her? Many adopted children, like Olga, have such thoughts.

The therapist's total attention to the patient during the therapy sessions allows the child to feel that the therapist is not just interested in the child but in his or her family, too. All children, independently of age and psychic symptoms, appreciate knowing that their parents are also receiving support and help. They can then concentrate more easily on their own working-through process. They do not have to worry anymore about how mum or dad is feeling.

Adults appreciate the help they receive and are especially keen to know how they best can talk to their children about what has afflicted the family. They wonder sometimes if it is not like rubbing salt in a wound to tell the children everything that has happened. Indeed, that was the thinking before, but not any longer. It is important to let children know the truth but it must be done in a careful way and in small doses.

Adults obviously cannot tell their children everything they have experienced, but they should be aware of the fact that children's fantasies are often much more frightening than reality. The situation of Ali's mother is especially difficult in this context. She was convinced that it would not help her or Ali to talk about her son's indirect war experiences, in other words, her trauma. In such cases the therapist should be humble and respect the parent's reservation. The therapist knows that the adult sooner or later will most probably have to put words to the so-called family secrets or other difficult experiences. This of course has to be done just as carefully, or more carefully, than was the case with information that was previously shared. Parents in these cases are usually surprised that their children already suspected or partly understood the nature of the secret all along.

Ideally, parents should get the kind of help that makes it possible for them to be the ones to tell their children about difficult experiences. It is important for children to find out about painful events from a person close to them. Everyone, children and adults, will always remember who delivered a painful message to them, where it happened and how it happened since they are extremely vulnerable in a situation like that and will remain so for a long time to come. The adult delivering the message has to be open and receptive and really listen so that the child will dare to ask questions about something he or she has never put into words before. Ronia finally dares to ask the forbidden question about how long her mother will be dead.

In order to strengthen children with a low self-esteem, the therapist uses a psychological approach that can most readily be compared to using a magnifying glass. The therapist searches painstakingly, as though through a magnifying glass, for everything that can be interpreted as positive about the child. This makes it possible to first find and then magnify those things that strengthen the child. It can be a trait, a talent, knowledge about something or a first step toward development in the child. During the work on giving the child a more positive self-image, the therapist helps the child dare to showcase positive things in an acceptable way of his or her own.

If the child hesitatingly shows the therapist something that he or she perhaps knows or can do, the therapist will magnify it by bringing it centre stage and shining a light on it. At that point children can be asked if they knew they had the showcased ability or knowledge. Often children are surprised and answer, just like Ali, that they had no clue about it. When it comes to children with internalizing symptoms, if they continue to have a difficult time acknowledging their abilities, society will continue to feel sorry for them. If they continue to evoke feelings of pity in people, people will deal with them inadequately and their development will be adversely affected. They will remain pitiful. The way Ronia was hindered in her development because of how people treated her is a perfect example of this phenomenon. That is why such children especially need the magnifying approach.

The most important goal in my work, as I have described it in this book, is naturally for children to gain good psychic health after the various interventions they have received. I have also wanted to describe and increase the general awareness of how short-term therapy is conducted. With my authentic narratives about work with traumatized children, I hope to increase the understanding of this therapeutic approach. Finally, I also hope that the narratives about Malte, Ronia, Olga, Ali and the work of Jenny, the psychologist, will strengthen the hope and the desire to help among those who have a chance to contribute seriously to the healing process in traumatized children.

Appendix I

Written agreement between parents and psychologist

Agreement

between

Name of parents and *Name of psychologist/psychotherapist*

Name of psychotherapist has carried out treatment in the form of short-term crisis therapy with our child, *Name of child*. She intends to write a book about working through crises with children. With this purpose in mind, she wishes to put together a manuscript with material from different therapies she has carried out, among them our child's therapy.

The aim of the book is to spread the knowledge that children who have had traumatic experiences at a young age can gain greatly from psychotherapeutic treatment. The therapist wishes to show how such treatment may ease psychic suffering, both in the present and for the future. The language used in the book will be down-to-earth and the psychological work will be described in a concrete manner. The reader will get a chance to follow children as they receive help in working through their traumas. The manuscript may be translated into other languages.

We, *Name of parents,* agree to let *Name of psychotherapist* use material from our child's treatment for publication in book form. We understand that the names of persons and places will be changed and that we have the right to read the completed manuscript and give our views. Once we have seen and approved the final manuscript, no further changes may be made without our consent.

We have been informed that *Name of psychotherapist* is bound by the law of confidentiality in her work as a mental health professional. The present agreement releases her from confidentiality in the clearly defined and limited context of the book referred to above.

Place and date:

Signature of parents
Address and telephone number

Signature of psychologist/psychotherapist
Name of clinic/institution

Appendix II

Written agreement between child and psychologist

Agreement

between

Name of child and *Name of psychologist/psychotherapist*

Name of child, who is X years old, goes to psychotherapy carried out by *Name of psychotherapist*, at *Name of clinic or institution. Name of psychotherapist* has said that she wants to write a book about *Name of child* and his/her therapy. He/she thinks this is a good idea. We have spoken many times now about the fact that *Name of psychotherapist* is going to write a book. *She* has also let *Name of child* know which things she does not want to tell about in the book.

Name of psychotherapist is keen to tell more people about child psychotherapy, people who do not know what psychotherapy is. She is happy that *Name of child* wants to help out. She wants more children and their mums and dads to get a chance at therapy. The book will be about children who have gone to psychotherapy carried out by *Name of psychotherapist.* She is going to use material from therapies with several different children.

Name of psychotherapist is bound by the code of confidentiality. This means that she is not allowed to tell others what someone has told her in therapy. But if a child and his/her mum and dad have given *Name of psychotherapist* permission to do so, she may be released from confidentiality. Therefore, the material that is used concerns only the children who have given their permission. *Name of child* has said that he/she wants to share his/her story. All names of persons and places will be changed. Only the children and the families involved will recognize themselves. *Name of dad* and *Name of mum* have also said that it is okay for *Name of psychotherapist* to write a book where material about *Name of child* is included. *Name of therapist for parents*, mum's and dad's therapist, has also said that she thinks the book is a good idea. It is a good way to tell about work at *Name of clinic or institution.*

Name of psychotherapist has written up this agreement so that we will remember the way we have thought about this book together. Mum, dad and their therapist are with us when we sign our names on two papers. *Name of child* and *Name of psychotherapist* get a signed paper each. We will put them in a safe place.

Place and date

Name of child *Name of psychologist/psychotherapist*

Index

Page numbers in italic format indicate figures and tables.